Don´t Take Their Faith for Granted

WAGNER MÉNDEZ

DON'T TAKE THEIR FAITH FOR GRANTED

Category: Spiritual/Religion/Motivational/Instruction

Copyright© 2023 Wagner Méndez
All rights reserved

ISBN: 9798376689219

Library of Congress Control Number: 2023902842
Independently Published

Author: Wagner Méndez

Cover image: iStock by Getty Images

Cover picture: Michael Sanchez, London

Unless otherwise stated, Scripture quotations are taken from the Holy Bible, New International Version®, NIV®.
Copyright © 1973, 1978, 1984, 2011 by Biblica, Inc. ®
Used by permission. All rights reserved worldwide

All rights reserved. No part of this publication may be reproduced, stored in a retrieval system, or transmitted, in any form or by any means, without prior permission in writing from the author.

To

Angel and Luz Martínez

Your great examples are very inspiring to me and to many other people around the world.

Acknowledgments

This English version of the original book *Que sus ejemplos no sean en vano* could not be ready for English speaking audience without the unique contribution of Mohan Nanjundan and Maggie Miller. Mohan and Maggie were like two angels I found in the West Region of the London International Church of Christ. They reviewed my original translation and polished it, to have this final version you have in your hands.

In addition to reviewing the English, they went the extra mile to edit it's content. Their suggestions made this book not only a new edition in English but also a new revised edition, which forces me to go back to the original to make a second one including all their insights. Thank you very much for all your time and energy put into helping me and, at the same time, helping many other people who will benefit from the book.

I would also like to acknowledge the support received from all my brothers and sisters here in London, especially in the West Region. Your support made my transition from the Dominican Republic to London easier. You also inspired me to find the time to translate the book into English to share it with all of you. Before coming here, I thought the collection of my good friends was already full. However, I realised that God has a perfect plan to help us to continue to build great friendships throughout our whole life. The friendships built in our church in London has been a great link in the chain of my life.

Contents

Acknowledgments vii

Foreword xi

Foreword to the Spanish Edition xiii

Introduction .... - 1 -

Ruth: The Path to Royalty .... - 3 -

Noah: Enter Through the Narrow Gate .... - 13 -

Job: Perseverance Through Suffering .... - 21 -

Daniel: A Fireproof Mancontinue .... - 29 -

Stephen: .... - 37 -

His Convictions Moved Jesus' Heart .... - 37 -

Abraham: An Unshakeable Faith .... - 43 -

Joseph: An Unconditional Love for God .... - 51 -

Isaac: God Blesses Obedience .... - 63 -

Jonathan: A Great Lesson of Love, Friendship, and Sacrifice for Humanity .... - 69 -

The Poor Widow: Practical Faith .... - 77 -

Cloud of Witnesses: Living Examples .... - 81 -

Fully Trusting in Your God .... - 95 -

ix

FOREWORD

Through the years I've seen Christians "begin their race" with a lot of promise. I've found that it is impossible to tell from the beginning who will do well in the years ahead, that is to say, who will "hear the word, retain it, and by persevering, produce a crop, thirty, sixty or a hundred times what was sown."

A bright start does not guarantee a good end, since some "receive the word at once with joy…but wither because they have no root." On the other hand, some come to the kingdom with little to offer, from a worldly point of view, but who genuinely love the Lord with a growing love, and who learn to walk with God and "grow in the grace and knowledge" of our Lord Jesus Christ. Thus, perseverance, understood as keeping your eyes fixed on Jesus, and not giving up, is a most important quality.

With this in mind, Wagner Mendez has given us this rich book, originally written in Spanish, full of biblical examples and testimonies of "real live" 21st-century disciples of Jesus Christ, as well as several examples from his own life. Wagner writes in a personable, conversational, and challenging style, offering questions for reflection at the end of each chapter. He is concerned to provide material that helps in our lives, rooted in Scripture.

Wagner is a dear friend, and he lives out a happy life of service in our congregation in West London. He laughs readily, is an open book with his life, and is always quick to volunteer help where it is needed. I am glad to commend his book to you. From Jesus' fullness, we have all received grace upon grace. Don't take it for granted!

Mohan Nanjundan
West Region
London International Church of Christ

FOREWORD TO THE SPANISH EDITION

First of all, I would like to let you know that reading is one of my good habits that take place not for emotion or for passion, but because I recognise the need to do it. But being honest, I confess that when I started reading the draft of this book, I quickly found myself almost halfway through it. Its reading is fresh, striking, and easy to connect with. I believe that just as happened to me, will also happen to many of the readers. They won't want to stop reading.

The book refers to biblical and living examples that we can follow. In these modern times that we are living, these examples become more and more difficult to find. It is difficult to find men and women who make a difference and a positive impact in our lives with their actions.

I don't know if you have noticed it. We often find ourselves talking about our grandparents or our great-grandparents as those who had an upright and exemplary walk in their lives. They were our role models from generation to generation. I am not saying that today it is impossible to find good examples in human beings. However, it does become increasingly difficult to find men and women who inspire us with their lives, their character, and their actions. And this occurs much more in the spiritual realm.

In this book "Don´t Take It for Granted", my friend and brother in Christ Wagner Méndez captures in a practical way, but at the same time digging deeper, the lives of men and women who were not perfect. In fact, we will be surprised to see the lives of some of them before knowing God. However, after they walked with God, their lives changed. At the same time, they are a strong inspiration for those of us who read these stories, not only with the intention of being mere spectators, but also as a call to be ourselves men and women of God who leave a good taste with our lives after leaving this world and, with it, we also leave a pleasant aroma of our walk with God, just as Christ Jesus, our Lord, did.

In the same way that these stories impacted me, inspired me to follow their examples, and to personally be an example to others, I hope they can do the same to you too. This world needs good social and spiritual examples. Let's not sit still without doing anything. Let's make a difference.

Yrán Fernández
Evangelist
Santo Domingo Church of Christ

INTRODUCTION

The Bible is full of inspiring examples that help us strengthen our relationship with God and persevere. Writing about each of these examples can lead us to make books larger than the Bible itself. Similar to what the Scriptures say about everything Jesus did, books could be written that would not fit in the whole world (John 21:25). However, only a few selected examples have been included in this book to help strengthen us and to deepen our spiritual convictions.

As with the first editions of many other books, with this one we begin with these examples, but it is very likely that others will be inserted in later editions to continue to inspire us more. When reading these examples if you think you have any other suggestion of another character or situation in the Bible that could be inspiring, please, feel free to make a suggestion to insert it.

The idea to write this book arose after writing the other one titled Beyond the Firmament: Persevering in Your Walk with God (In Spanish). Most of this material comes from the third part of that book. Because of its volume, I wanted to make smaller books based on the different parts of that first one. Here I leave this titled "Don´t Take It for Granted." My plan is to publish two others. One of them is about basic principles to understand the fundamentals of the Christian life and the other is about various obstacles that we must overcome in our walk with God.

I have seen that some people measure the quality of a book by its volume. If it is not very voluminous, they consider it to be a good book. Because of the size, people think it is easier to read. Well, I can also include myself in that group. Sometimes we see a bulky book and it challenges us to read it. But there are also many other people who are not concerned about the size of the book but about its content. In this book, I make a combination for all kinds of audiences who are looking for inspiration to strengthen themselves spiritually. This is not a very big book, but it contains inspiring examples of great Bible heroes that are still alive in our minds today. I do not want these examples to replace the original source, the Bible, where the stories of these characters are found. Rather, the goal is for people who read this book to return to the original source to learn more about them.

For many of these people, the book provides a perspective on them that is often not heard or read about in other sources. Sometimes writers and preachers focus on strengthening the same perspective on each other. Emphasising these perspectives is good since each of us must always remember things previously learned, but also when we share other perspectives, it helps us to have another vision that also strengthens us. Sometimes the Spirit puts in us the idea to write and share something and we miss the opportunity. In this case, I did not want to make that mistake. I prefer to let myself be led by the Spirit and share what he has inspired me to do. Sometimes we also consider that our ideas are not that important, but when others read them, they feel inspired and their comments also inspire us to keep writing. With my other books, I have helped other people, and they have also been of great benefit and have strengthened me.

My expectation is that this book will inspire you and that you will be a multiplier inspiring other. Just as the Scriptures inspire us to help other people come to Jesus, I hope these teachings can be used to help other people follow those examples. Let us seek to have the same convictions as these people and let us be instruments to continue to help these examples remain alive in our hearts and for humanity, which needs it so much to face the growing challenges of life.

When I wrote my first spiritual book, Beyond the Firmament, I thought I was doing it to help other people. Later I realised that it was also a great help for me when I went through the most challenging situation in my life. I was kidnapped in Haiti, and about that situation, I may write another book. All my belongings were stolen, including my Bible and my computer. I was also tortured. In that situation, that first book and its examples were key to keeping my focus on the Scriptures and having a good attitude despite the difficult time I was going through. Just days before that situation, I had devotional times with God on the examples that I had written about. That strengthened me, and even though I thought I was not going to survive, I kept my trust in God.

I hope you can get inspired by these examples and that we continue to exalt and glorify the name of our God.

1

Ruth: The Path to Royalty

"But Ruth replied, "Don't urge me to leave you or to turn back from you. Where you go I will go, and where you stay I will stay. Your people will be my people and your God my God."

- *RUTH 1:16*

The focus of this chapter could be twofold. It could be double even if the name is only one: Ruth. On the one hand, it could focus on Ruth, the Moabite. But, on the other hand, also, without any doubt for me, and I believe that many other people who knew her would agree, it could focus on Ruth Espinal, the Dominican disciple who never lost her convictions despite the suffering and the persecution.

Every one of us who is still alive is fighting to persevere until the end being faithful to God. I have written this book with this in mind, thinking that I have persevered. I have done it up to this point, but Ruth Espinal did it until the day she died. She never lost her convictions. But first let me focus on Ruth, the Moabite, whom I told you about originally. Then I talk about Ruth Espinal.

Throughout the Bible, we see many examples of people who have inspired us. Sometimes we are inspired when we hear a message preached. We take the teachings to our hearts and they strengthen our convictions. Ruth's case is something very special to me. Her convictions have impacted me enormously. Even though my wife and I have many disagreements in terms of opinions (and are we different from other couples?), we did agree that Ruth 1:16 was the scripture to use for our wedding invitation. I also think that my convictions about this book did not come from hearing any message, but that God put it directly into my heart. I should also mention that Ralph Ojeda, one of the ministers who instructed me in Puerto Rico, once told me that original ideas arise when we forget who taught us them.

Let's see all the teachings that we can learn from Ruth's convictions and that could help us persevere in our walk with God. These can take us to places and situations that we have never imagined before. Writing about this is like a dream come true for me. I have preached on Ruth's convictions before and was looking forward to having the opportunity to one day put this in a book.

Before going directly to see Ruth's convictions, and as a basis for the discussion, let's see why Naomi's family moved from Ephrata (Bethlehem) to Moab. Moab may not sound very familiar to us, but if we say Moabites, maybe yes. We remember that the Moabites were not people of royal lineage and on whom God was focused. The Moabites, along with the Ammonites, come from Lot and from the fruit of the incest relationship with his daughters (Genesis 19: 31-38).

As described at the beginning of the book of Ruth, Elimelek, a man from Bethlehem of Judah, went to live in Moab because of the famine that was in the region at the time when Israel was ruled by judges (caudillo). Please pay close attention to this. The only reason mentioned why Elimelek went to live in Moab was because of the famine. It wasn't because the mission in Moab needed him or because of his special plan to evangelise the Moabites.

Possibly this was a unilateral decision by him without seeking any advice or without consulting his family to see if they agreed. Possibly he just followed his heart's desires. I can understand that the husband at home has a provider approach and wants to do whatever it takes to support his family. I can relate with him in that regard, but decisions shouldn't be made based only on that. There are many other aspects to consider, especially the spiritual one.

Later, we can see the results of that decision. Elimelek died in Moab. His two sons also died. We also see that his economic situation did not improve. If it had improved, Naomi might not have had to return to Bethlehem. His situation definitely worsened, leaving his family helpless.

DON'T TAKE THEIR FAITH FOR GRANTED

What lesson can we learn from that situation? I have learned my lesson in advance without having to go through that situation. In my heart is the strong conviction not to move from where I am with the church only for merely financial reasons. I will not move to improve my economic situation without focusing on providing greater support to the kingdom and giving my heart more to God. I have seen some people make that decision and, although they may improve financially, their spiritual situation gets worse. In other cases, even their economic situation also worsens.

Ruth had such Deep convictions that her impact will last for eternity.

Moving on to our focus on Ruth, let me ask you why the book is called Ruth and not Naomi. Doesn't Naomi have enough credits for a book in the Bible to be named after her? Didn't Naomi play a good leading role with her convictions? It may be. But what Ruth did was extraordinary. Ruth's convictions were so deep that her impact has been marked throughout history.

In addition, I would like to mention the case of another woman with deep convictions. Do you know the name of Naomi's other daughter-in-law who was with Ruth when Naomi returned to Bethlehem? Is her name mentioned anywhere else in the Bible? Didn't she also have enough merits so that history continues to remember her? Possibly yes.

Orpah may have been a woman of deep convictions as well. That's why Naomi had to beg her to stay. I personally think she did the right thing at that time. She responded to a legitimate request from Naomi. Naomi felt good about that. But let's see Ruth again. She has no comparison. Ruth made an impact with her deep convictions, and God blessed her beyond expectations. Ruth did not let herself be overcome by Naomi's request. She was so grateful to Naomi that she was willing to suffer, leave her gods, and even die to always be with her mother-in-law.

It is highly possible that Naomi's husband and their sons, Mahlon and Kilion, also did their part in making an impact on Ruth so that she would be so grateful to her mother-in-law. What a difference compared to situations nowadays where in the world mothers-in-law are despised so much and are even mocked!

Each of us must imitate Ruth's convictions. Ruth did not allow herself to be discouraged by her mother-in-law to change her mind about her gratitude and her desire to follow her. She kept her convictions until the end. On many occasions, we act with strong convictions, but we do not persevere until the end. We persevere until almost the end, and then when things get too tough, we gave up. We feel that we do have an excuse to give up. And we don't take responsibility for our weaknesses. On the contrary, what we do is blame others or the circumstances around us for the situation we are facing.

> *The fact that we are followers of Jesus should help us be excellent in our Jobs imitating him.*

Ruth kept her convictions to the end. She said: "—¡"*But Ruth replied, "Don't urge me to leave you or to turn back from you. Where you go I will go, and where you stay I will stay. Your people will be my people and your God my God. Where you die I will die, and there I will be buried. May the Lord deal with me, be it ever so severely, if even death separates you and me."* (Ruth 1:16-17). When Naomi saw Ruth's convictions, she had no choice but to give up. Then they left and went to Bethlehem.

Did Ruth know what awaited her in the future? No. She didn't really expect anything. She was simply willing to accept what Naomi's God, now her God, had for her.

Many times, our expectations of receiving something that benefits us are so high that we receive a lot, but we are not happy. We look forward to getting much more. If our expectations are to always accept God's will, it is possible that we receive little and think that what we receive is a lot. Ruth really did get a lot without expecting it, regardless of which point of view we look at it.

What did Ruth expect? Did she expect to marry again? Did she expect to marry someone super special? Possibly not. She was simply willing to trust God and accept his will (Proverbs 16:3, Psalms 137:4, Proverbs 21:1).

In addition to her convictions and appreciation for her mother-in-law, Ruth was a very hard-working woman. This characteristic becomes a great complement to her convictions and her faithfulness. God is looking for that kind of heart. Her attitude towards work led her to be noticed by a hard-working and exemplary man. Today, unfortunately, the image of the religious world is not that people are hard workers. It is an image that after people decide to follow Jesus, they become careless about work. They want to leave everything to God.

Fortunately, that was not what I saw in the congregation of which I became a member in Puerto Rico and with which I also went as a missionary to the Dominican Republic. On the contrary, since the beginning when someone wants to come to the kingdom, we focus on helping the person to work and not to be a burden to the church. We perfectly understand the scripture in which Paul tells us that *"The one who is unwilling to work shall not eat."* (2 Thessalonians 3:10).

> *Ruth was not a burden for Naomi. On the other hand, Ruth took care of her.*

Paul didn't just say it. He was also an example of focusing on working and not on being a burden to the church. He had the right to be supported by the church for his work, but he chose to continue with his job of tent-making (Acts 18:3, 2 Thessalonians 3:6-9). Furthermore, in different parts of the Bible, including Proverbs, reference is made to working. This means that when we decide to follow Jesus, if we neglect to work, this is a very simple vague excuse and a pure religiosity without any impact on other people around us.

The fact that we follow Jesus should help us to be excellent in our jobs by imitating him. Jesus was the son of God, and he was also a carpenter (Mark 6:3). It is said that he was not a simple carpenter, but that he was a master. As Alfonso Lockward's New Bible Dictionary says (1992, p. 571), Jesus had a great capacity for learning, demonstrated by being recorded in the incident in Luke 2:41-52, when Jesus was lost and his parents found him sitting in the midst of the teachers of the law listening to them and asking questions. With that capacity and knowing the perfection of Jesus, it is not possible that in his job he was going to allow himself to be less than excellent and not set the best example.

Ruth was not a burden to Naomi. On the contrary, Ruth sacrificed herself for her. She worked to help herself and Naomi too. It wasn't Naomi who sent her to work. She asked Naomi to let her go to work. And since God blesses those who are faithful to him, he was preparing the way for her to go to work in the right place, the field of Boaz, a relative of Elimelek. Later, seeing Ruth's hard work, Boaz decided to marry her. But first, he decided to comply with all the established procedures, as a righteous man like him would do. And please don't stop. Continue to read and you will see what God did through that marriage and the eternal impact of Ruth because of her strong convictions.

> *Ruth, a Moabite, became a part of Jesus ancestries.*

Ruth's convictions are truly impressive. But even more impressive are the blessings of God as a result of those convictions. Ruth, a Moabite, became one of the ancestors of Jesus (Matthew 1:5). This is almost impossible to believe. A Moabite, belonging to a tribe despised by God. That is why I have titled this chapter "Ruth: The Path to Royalty."

There are many other lessons we can learn in addition to Ruth's convictions. We see that God focuses on the heart of a person without considering the background, race, or appearance (1 Samuel 16:7, Deuteronomy 10:16-19, James 2:1). Let's keep in mind that God seeks those hearts regardless of the country, church, or social class. If you have a heart for God, he will show you the right path and his church where you can give him glory and honour.

It is possible that you feel that your congregation is not doing everything that it should do for God according to what the Scriptures say. And this leads me to think about everything described by David Platt in his book "Radical"[1]. You don't have to be bitter. You can make a difference through the Scriptures. I was in that situation before becoming a disciple of Jesus, and I did not stop. I studied the Scriptures and realised that many of the things they taught me, even without being a committed disciple of Jesus, were not what the Bible said. They taught me religiousness, but not convictions for God.

And what happened to the other Moabites? Possibly they continued to worship their gods. I don't know if Ruth had the opportunity to look back and help her family to also follow her new God, the true God. What we do know is about the impact she had on the future because of her convictions.

---

[1] Platt, David (2010). Radical: Taking Back Your Faith from the American Dream. Multnomah Books.

Someone may also wonder why Boaz, her husband, had the honour of being part of the genealogy of Jesus. Truly, in addition to being a righteous man, Boaz also came from a genealogy of someone who made an impact and touched the heart of God. Do you know who Boaz's mother was? She was the great Rahab, the prostitute. Excuse me, Wagner, and where is the impact? As a friend of mine once said: "Wagner, I thought you were a spiritual man." Yes, that prostitute was the one who protected the spies who went to explore the promised land. It was also not expected that Rahab could make an eternal impact. But she was a woman of convictions and chosen by God for that great purpose. God also promises great blessings to our future generations when we are righteous people. Those promises were made to Abram (Abraham), Noah, David, and many others (Genesis 12:7, Deuteronomy 28:1-14, 2 Samuel 7).

> *Let us be people of Deep convictions for our God.*

Let us be people of deep convictions for our God. Let's seek to make a difference with our own convictions no matter what is happening around us. The story is not over yet. The number of people who are following God with all their hearts today is very small compared to the size of the population. God wants people of deep convictions to make a big impact. Nothing limits us to do it. We admire Jesus' example, but he said that if we believe in him, we can do even greater things than he did (John 14:12-14). Let's be people with deep convictions and persevere in our walk with God for his glory and honour.

And as I mentioned at the beginning and I mention again, we can see the testimony of Ruth Espinal and her perseverance until the very end of her life. Ruth was the first member of her blood family to radically decide to follow Jesus as the Scriptures say and be a true disciple. This led her to receive strong persecution from her family. But her righteousness and perseverance, also helped her sister Tati to become a disciple later when my wife Guarina studied the Bible with her. And that later, her brother-in-law, Emilio, also became a disciple. And that later, his niece Carolina, the eldest daughter of Emilio and Tati, also became a disciple. And I am confident that in the future she will also do so with her other son, Emilio, Jr. And the seed is sown so that her other brothers and sisters, who have already visited the church, do so too.

Family persecution of Ruth, and possibly our church, worsened when Ruth developed nervous problems, which seem to run in her family. When that happened, the family thought it was because of her radical focus on following Jesus. And it is not strange. Jesus' family also thought the same thing. Despite her health situation, Ruth did not lose her convictions. Nor did her sister Tati and her brother-in-law Emilio. On the contrary, their convictions were strengthened.

> *God wants people of deep convictions to make a big impact.*

Ruth's health situation worsened due to the contamination of bacteria in the medical centre where she was. By God's mercy and all our prayers, when we thought that Ruth was not going to survive, God healed her and allowed her to live, although she was left with mobility problems and with many other limitations. God gave her the opportunity to share her testimony with us and leave a written testimony of her as well. Later, when we thought we were going to have her for a long time, God thought it was better to take her to live with him. Ruth herself died at the tender age of 32, on November 8, 2008. But she left us her testimony that despite all the suffering we go through, we could persevere in our walk with God until the end. And Ruth could with deep convictions say: *"I have fought the good fight, I have finished the race, I have kept the faith. 8 Now there is in store for me the crown of righteousness, which the Lord, the righteous Judge, will award to me on that day—and not only to me, but also to all who have longed for his appearing."* (2 Timothy 4:7-8).

In her time of illness, Ruth began to take notes to write a book with her testimony that could help many other people even after her death. Apart from other things that she wrote and that I do not have at hand, she wrote the following:

What You Need to Be Happy
By Ruth Espinal (1976-2008)

Thank God for everything he gives you, no matter how small and insignificant it may seem.
Live each day with enthusiasm.
Celebrate a Christmas inside you every month of the year.
Always keep in mind that you are going to have good days and bad days.
When something makes you sad, repeat "this also shall pass".
Enjoy everything you can do, even the act of drinking a glass of water.
Make a commitment to mention only the good qualities of each person.
Appreciate what life gives you because that is what belongs to you.
Give a smile to everyone who approaches you.
Discover the divine purpose in everything that happens to you.
Eliminate every complaint in your life from its root.
Look at the sky during the day and during the night to contemplate its beauty.
Remember [that] things are not always going to be as you expect them to be.
Accept the disease patiently and rejoice, because the care of God and people will overflow you.
Love yourself, because nobody is going to do it better than you.
Fill your mind with positive and encouraging thoughts. Don't give destructive thoughts a chance.
Listen to music that feeds your spirit and warms your heart.
Free yourself from feelings of guilt that prevent you from living peacefully.
Reflect and meditate on your life at the end of each day so that you can be a better person.
Become an optimistic person who looks for a way out of everything.
Make sure you have someone to talk to about your fears, anxieties, and frustrations.
....And remember.
Happiness is within you. Therefore, it depends on you to be happy.

Both, in the Bible and in living examples, we can have testimonies of radical people who have persevered in their walk with God and have set a great example for us. We have the two Ruth. Ruth, the Moabite, a biblical example, and Ruth Espinal, an example that we saw living with us. Let's take these and other examples to strengthen our convictions and persevere in our walk with God until the very end to continue to leave an example for eternity.

TO REFLECT

1. Simply, what is your conviction for your God? What are you willing to do to persevere in your walk with God?

2. Decide to do something radical for God that can make an eternal impact.

3. What price would make you change your convictions about God?

4. What obstacle in the way could make you deviate and not persevere?

II

Noah: Enter Through the Narrow Gate

"Enter through the narrow gate. For wide is the gate and broad is the road that leads to destruction, and many enter through it. But small is the gate and narrow the road that leads to life, and only a few find it".

- *MATHEW 7:13-14*

In this life, it is very simple just to follow the flow and do what most people are doing or have done. Swimming against the tide is similar to the teaching of Jesus about entering through the narrow gate. Most people throughout history, and to this day, have simply followed the flow. They have followed the convictions of the majority.

Swimming against the tide is very difficult. It is easier to get pulled by the flow without making any effort. It is also easier to follow the majority and seek their approval than to stand by your convictions for God despite peer pressure. Noah was a man who swam against the flow. His impact was so great that I can affirm that without him humanity could not even exist today (Genesis 6: 5).

Currently, it seems that sin and wickedness are increasing in the world. And what I see scares me. Crime is increasing and it seems that it is difficult to control it. It is even seen that evil grows faster than the number of people who are willing to transform their lives. The number of people who are willing to do good seems to grow at a slower rate than those who are determined to do bad things on purpose. Added to this are people who are not willing to transform their lives thinking that what they are doing is right. In addition, there are also those who would like to do what is right and do not do it because of all the confusion that exists in the world about truth and lies.

Since the beginning, God has seen that man was always thinking about doing evil (Genesis 6:5). Even if we go a little further back, we also see how man was controlled by emotions, the desire for greatness, and the deception of Satan through a simple serpent (Genesis 2).

God is not blind to what is happening in the world. He is God. Because of the so much evil that existed, God wanted to erase the man he had created from the earth. He wanted to destroy his artistic masterpiece. Can you imagine what it can cost you and the time you have to invest in creating an art masterpiece? How would you feel about going through the process of having to destroy it because it has deviated from its original purpose?

> *In spite of all the bad things happening in the world at that time, Noah was a good man who always obeyed God. He decided to swim against the flow.*

"*But Noah found favour in the eyes of the Lord.*" (Genesis 6:8). Noah was the person who brought relief to God. Noah saved humanity from being totally destroyed. In spite of all the bad things happening in the world at that time, Noah was a good man who always obeyed God. He decided to go against the grain. He did not follow the convictions of other people around him.

In my particular case, I always repeat something that had a great impact on me when I studied the Bible to become a disciple in Puerto Rico. The focus was on teaching me to create my own convictions through the Scriptures and not just to follow other people's convictions. Those deep convictions have helped me persevere in my walk with God despite all the difficult situations I have had to face. It has also been difficult to see so much disinterest of people on following God around me.

Is it that Puerto Rico has something special, but not the Dominican Republic? No. Puerto Rico, like the Dominican Republic and many other countries, is a country full of religiousness and not too many people who are willing to sacrifice to follow Jesus and give their lives for him if necessary. This is shown by the fact that if you take a survey of the number of people who are Christians, you find that more than 90 percent say they are. However, this does not explain why most people have to live behind bars as if they were imprisoned.

The difference was not really made by the country. The difference was made by a group of people committed to following God and willing to always obey him, according to the instructions of the Bible. When we obey God's instructions, we make a difference and have an eternal impact. God looks for people who obey him. Despite the wickedness at the beginning, Noah remained faithful. When God asked Noah to build the boat, *"Noah did everything just as God commanded him."* (Genesis 6:22, 7:5). Do you see the point? Following instructions is often very difficult. Many times, our emotions control us. We usually seek to put our personal seal on what we do, and we try to justify why we should do it that way. We want to pretend that we know more than God.

When we obey God's instructions, we make a difference and have an eternal impact.

To find a man like Noah who lived according to his commands and that was willing to obey him was always a great joy to God. This was also a great blessing for mankind. I say that creation could have been affected if it hadn't been for Noah. God is always ready to start over again and, for his great love, he is willing to give the lives of other people and to destroy nations to protect those who love him (Isaiah 43:4). He demonstrated it with Noah and he continued to do it throughout history.

God looks for people who are faithful to him and to protect them he does whatever it takes. God's love is so immense that sometimes it is difficult for us to understand it. If we do not dig deeper into the Scriptures, we will not understand his great love. Possibly many people see the destruction with the flood as a cruel act of God. However, God did it to show his love for someone who obeyed him. Noah was willing to persevere in his purpose, even though he did not see the immediate result. He did it out of obedience to God. God wants obedience instead of any sacrifice (1 Samuel 15:22).

What happened with Noah should serve as the basis for always being willing to obey God's instructions. However, many people simply want to follow their emotions and their desires of the heart and are fooled by them. To persevere in our walk with God we need to be radical. Just like Noah, there are also many examples of radical people who have decided to swim against the tide to persevere in doing what pleases God. Throughout this book, we will continue to look at various other examples.

> *Noah was willing to persevere in his purpose, even though he did not see the immediate result, out of obedience to God.*

In the history of mankind, no one person who has decided to go with the flow entering the wider gate has ever made such an extraordinary impact. The people who have made an impact have been those who have decided to go against established standards that do not please God. In addition, to keep the focus on doing what pleases God and to help the church to continue to do what it should do as the body of Christ, we need leaders with convictions. We need leaders who do not get overwhelmed by all the difficult situations that arise in their daily life and stay focused on doing what God wants.

The daily life situations that we have to face are so many that if we focus on solving them all with our individual means and resources, we would not have time to do anything else. You have to face them in a spiritual way and always apply the basic principles. This is why prayer in our walk with God is so important. There are things that are impossible to face on our own. We need to rely on the power of God.

I have a personal conviction about doing what is right. We do need to learn what God wants from us through his word and we must be willing to obey it. But my conviction is also that when we decide to be righteous seeking to do good and not just letting us be controlled by our emotions, God works in our favour and leads us in the direction he likes so that we learn more about how to live according to his will. He puts understanding in our hearts and gives us the ability to choose between good and bad. When we don't do it, many times it's not because we don't know, but because we don't want to do it.

Even without being a disciple of Jesus, when I entered the Higher Institute of Agriculture to study agriculture in 1982, I had to swim against the tide in order to survive as a student and not be expelled because of academic deficiency. This happened to about half of my classmates. They simply focused on following the what the majority was doing. We were a total of 65 students and only 33 graduated.

I swam against the tide to maintain my convictions in the search for excellence. My first year was very difficult. I thought I was not going to survive. Although I was not the youngest of the group, I was the smallest and the youngest in terms of body development. I was 16 years old, but I was still a child in every sense of the word. It was easy to do just what other more experienced people did. But my conviction was to totally focus on what I wanted, to graduate with a bachelor's degree in agricultural sciences from the famous Higher Institute of Agriculture. I didn't want to go back to my little hometown, El Estero, without my degree.

But my focus was not limited to simply graduating. I was focused on academic excellence as I define it in my book on that subject. I wanted to create a solid foundation for the future. I think I made it. The three years that I spent in high school transformed me from a boy to a man and from a rebel and disobedient child to a person of deep convictions and responsibility. (But please do not ask my wife about this as she may say that I am still in that stage of my life). I understand that God also saw my heart and he understood that I had all the resources to be a disciple or, at least, he began to shape my heart for that purpose.

The point is that I went against the grain by not following people who, even knowing the rules, violated them. I went against people who during study hours focused on wasting their time. Many people did not survive and had to be dropped out of the training program. In my case, my approach was to confront these people although I earned a bad reputation among my peers, simply because I was focusing on being responsible. I was inspired, and also terrified, by the idea of going back to my hometown if I got kicked out of high school.

While I was just like any other student at first, by the end of the first semester I was one of the students in the honour society. I continued to have that honour distinction in each one of the semesters and at the end of the three years of the training program, I was one of two honour students recognized at graduation. Like me, the other honour student also became a disciple years later, but he got caught up in life's situations and did not persevere in his walk with God. What an honour it was for me to help him become a disciple. But it was also painful to see him abandon God and lose the main battle in his life.

Facing my classmates, many times without any wisdom and being rude, trying to get them to focus on following the rules, caused many of them, literally, to hate me. I cannot justify my actions. There were many things that could have been better on my part. But the point I want to express is the one of going against the grain to achieve personal goals and glorify God. You cannot simply follow the flock and jeopardize persevering in your walk with God.

Going back to Noah, when he decided to obey God and build the ark, he may have been the laughingstock of most. Ha ha ha….. is this man going crazy? Building a ship in the desert? Noah was in Mount Ararat.

The same also happens today with the disciples of Jesus and it also happened with Jesus and his apostles. They thought Jesus was crazy. For many, his sacrifice on the cross was foolishness (1 Corinthians 1:18). But just as Noah's ark was salvation for him and his family, the cross is the power of God for those of us who understand and are willing to follow Jesus and to swim against the flow.

Today many people continue to follow the majority simply because it is the majority. Many continue to seek to enter the wider gate without making a sacrifice to enter through the narrow one. Other people simply continue in their sin, as in the days of Noah, ignoring God's warnings (Matthew 24:37, Luke 17:26). Those of us who have faith, as Noah had (Hebrews 11:7), will see something similar come true when Jesus returns, even if it is from afar.

I can write a lot more about Noah, but if I do, I think it will be pouring rain. It will be unnecessary. We can take the references from Genesis and many other writings about him to learn more details about this great man of God. What I do want us to understand is that, like Noah, we must be willing to go against the grain to stay faithful to God and to be an example to those around us.

I am reminded of a sister in Christ in the Dominican Republic. Her name is Eléxida González. She has stood firm in her walk with

God. Due to her faithfulness and perseverance, today she can have a husband, Isaías De Luna, who has also decided to follow Jesus and persevere. Today there are many people who have received help from them because of their love, their faith, and their perseverance. Let's imitate the example of Noah. Let's go against the grain to persevere and give glory to our God.

TO REFLECT

1. Do you think that doing what most people do can make an impact in life?

2. Are you willing to imitate people of convictions like Noah or Jesus and go against the grain even if you have to pay the price of loneliness? Doing so will reward you with blessings beyond expectations.

3. Put yourself in Noah's shoes. If it were your situation, would you follow God's plan and his instructions?

III

Job: Perseverance Through Suffering

"Should we accept only good things from the hand of God and never anything bad?"

- *JOB 2:10 (NLT)*

In our spiritual lives we may go through very challenging situations. In the Bible, we have many examples that strengthen our faith by seeing how people have overcome. We also make comparisons with other people who are facing the same situation today or with ourselves and decide to write about that to inspire others.

Job challenges each one of us. His level of suffering is unique. I think that in this entire chapter I will have to focus only on describing his situation without using any live story to compare with it. It is almost impossible to find a similar situation of human suffering. It's almost like seeing the sufferings of Jesus in an ordinary person.

I ask if I can find any testimony from someone who has gone through a similar test. Will I be able to relate myself with what Job went through to support and give more weight to what I write? I doubt it. Let's just learn the lessons of Job's suffering, his faithfulness to God, his convictions, and the reactions of "friends" around him, including his wife.

Anyone who wants to give personal testimony about the sufferings they have gone through similar to Job's will fall short. In each of these chapters, I try to find living testimonies and use my own experience for inspiration, but comparing myself to Job's suffering is a real challenge. Aside from Jesus, we do not find anyone who has suffered physically and emotionally as Job did. In spite of his suffering, Job persevered in his walk with God. Because of his faithfulness, God was always with him in his suffering and blessed him again beyond what we can imagine.

Let us keep in mind that everything that happens in this world is caused or allowed by God. God is in control of the smallest details in this world (Matthew 10:29). We may not understand why certain events happen, but God is in control. Sometimes we face very painful situations that can even lead us to lose our faith in God. However, it does not matter how much pain we feel, we must trust that God knows what he is doing.

In spite of his suffering, Job persevered in his walk with God.

An example that I usually give to people when they are going through painful situations is that if God shows us a video of the alternative course of life that would have happened without the pain, it would be scary. What happens in life, even if we don't understand it, is the best for those who love God (Romans 8:28). And God really works for the good of those who love him. We can lose a loved one in unexpected situations, but God does it because he thinks it's the best. These situations happen either to shape our hearts or, in my opinion, to prevent a future catastrophe.

Let us think, for example, about a child who dies. It causes great pain to his relatives. God could say that if the child had not died, the child could have caused a fire in which his entire house was going to be burned, the whole family would die, and other neighbouring houses would burn down as well. What do you think about this?

I remember once in the early 90s when I was studying in the United States. There was a children's program on Univision titled "Carousel". It was like a children's novel and I liked watching it. One day the children went to church to pray for the health of teacher Jimena, who had an accident. But there was a boy who decided not to go. Everyone went to the church except him. When asked why he didn't go, he replied that the night her grandmother died, he spent the whole night praying and, in spite of his prayer, God didn't stop her from dying. Hearing that from a child's voice moved me deeply. Sometimes we don't understand God's plans. Finally, after the others arrived at the church, the boy also arrived, and it was a great joy for all of them. If I remember correctly, I think the teacher didn't die.

This is how we react many times. We pray and we don't necessarily see the prayer answered at that moment. But that doesn't mean that God doesn't hear our prayers. He listens and answers them. What happens is that what we think is not necessarily the way God thinks (Isaiah 55:8). God thinks differently from the way we think. God does not adapt himself to the way we think. We need to mature spiritually to get closer to the way God thinks and acts. The more we mature spiritually, the more we will understand it. This is achieved by persevering in our walk with God.

Let's start at the beginning of the account of the story of Job and see what happened. Job was a very rich man and very faithful to God. God was very pleased with him. He was a very righteous man. But do you think Satan likes that? No. When Satan sees someone like him and that through that person others are going to get closer to God, he points all his guns at him and looks for a way to destroy him. He wanted to destroy Job, but he couldn't do it. Job had a very solid relationship with God and he did not let anything or anyone affect it.

Satan looked at Job and thought that his faithfulness to God was based on his possessions. He thought that if God took away everything he had, including his health, Job would deny God. The first attack he made on Job was to take away his possessions one by one. How would you feel if you suddenly lost all your material possessions right now? Sometimes we put our trust in the riches of this world. God warns us that our confidence should not be based on riches, but on being righteous (Proverbs 11:28). Job understood this perfectly and it was his life style. Job was a righteous and faultless man before God (Job 1:1).

How would you feel if you suddenly lose all your material possessions right now?

Job received a series of four disastrous pieces of news about losing material possessions until he was left with nothing. In addition, he also lost his family. How would you react in that situation? Would you say you can relate to Job? Despite all of that, Job's focus was on trusting God and acknowledging that God had given him everything and that God had taken everything away (Job 1:21). Job's focus was also on praising God and on staying free from sin. Again, I ask if anyone can relate to this, to lend me a bit of their faith!

Before we continue, let's look at everything God says about focusing on the riches and material possessions of this world. If we stick to the things of this world, we will suffer. There is always the possibility of losing material possessions, either by the actions of Satan or by God's decision to test and strengthen our character. Not only should we not stick to the riches of this world as I mentioned earlier, but we should make good use of them. Like David in Psalm 119:14, Job rejoiced more in being faithful to God by obeying his commands than in the riches he had. Job also made good use of his wealth to help other people in need (Job 29:12).

Job's true wealth was his love for God and his righteousness. What is your wealth? I consider that my heart is set on being righteous to God and on doing whatever it takes to persevere, but I must also recognise the desire to have extra income to solve my financial commitments and to live without debts and to avoid selling my assets.

If we stick to things of this world, we will suffer.

Today, the love for the riches of this world is something that greatly affects whether a person perseveres in his walk with God. Sometimes we focus too much on getting more and more. And those who have a lot let themselves be dominated by keeping that wealth and do not focus on God. It is difficult today to find a person with the riches that Job had and whose main focus is on being righteous to God. The Bible tells us that it is *"Better to be lowly in spirit along with the oppressed than to share plunder with the proud"* (Proverbs 16:19). That really is a temptation, but Job did not fall on it.

In my particular case, being a person who had practically nothing, many times I have felt that inner struggle. Do I humble myself with the poor or try to get closer to those who have more to show that I belong to that social class? Am I going to play basketball with the disciples or am I going to play golf with a class where I don't belong and that I want to insert myself to show my pride?

I give thanks to God that, after being a disciple, he has allowed me to enjoy the blessings of having a group of friends younger than me. I say this because, due to my age and the academic environment in which I grew up, the tendency was to be part of an older group and current executives from different companies. However, I have built such incredible relationships with a group of young people that when I came to the church as a professional and college professor, they were still students. Today these young professionals are my great friends, who challenge me spiritually and professionally to give more to God and to society. Going through that process has been wonderful. Continuing with my old friends from around the world was only going to increase my arrogance, thinking that I was the best in the world with all the compliments I received.

Continuing with Job, how would you feel if you received the first pieces of news that he received, the second, the third, and the fourth, consecutively? Many of us don't even bear one and stay faithful in our walk with God. When Satan saw Job's courage, I imagine his teeth gnashed and his attack intensified. He didn't just focus on taking away all his possessions, he also asked God to allow him to take away his health. He said that Job was faithful because what he lost did not touch his skin directly. But God knew what a fighting cock he had. God knew that Job would remain faithful regardless of what happened to him.

Possibly God gave what he gave Job because he knew that he would know how to manage it and how to keep his heart focused without being led astray by the deceitfulness of riches. Sometimes we ask God for riches and other material and non-material things and God does not give them to us because God knows that if we receive them, they will harm us (James 4:2).

When Job lost his health, it was very painful physically and emotionally. Satan knows human nature very well, but different from God, his intelligence is limited. He thought that if Job lost his health, after having lost all his material possessions and his family, he would deny God. With God's permission, Satan sent a disease upon Job that covered his skin from head to toe (Job 2:7). That was really painful. But even more painful was when you are going through a situation of this nature and you don't have anyone to help you.

I imagine that in that moment of suffering, Job wanted to find the support of his wife. But he did not receive it. His wife was really cruel to him. She said to him: *"Are you still trying to maintain your integrity? Curse God and die."* (Job 2:9). How would you react in such a situation? Tell me. And again, lend me some of your good reactions and faith.

Knowing my emotional nature and that I expect a lot from other people, I cannot imagine how I would have reacted. What I know is that my reaction might not have pleased God. Job, on the contrary, as he always did, reacted with his characteristic reaction of a faithful man with a big heart for God when he said: *"You talk like a foolish woman. Should we accept only good things from the hand of God and never anything bad?"* (Job 2:10). The Bible also says that despite everything that happened to Job, he did not sin even with words. What thoughts would you have had or what words would you have spoken in such circumstances? Possibly, because of my nature, my words would not have been bad, but I am sure that my thoughts would have been unpublishable.

Later come the "super friends". Now come those who are going to comfort Job in this moment of anguish: the "super spiritual". Do you want to have some friends like them? I give them to you as a gift. I don't want them.

Unfortunately, sometimes we find this type of people, whose religiosity leads them to try to appear super spiritual in any circumstance, but with a heart as hard as the hardest wood. His friends swore that Job was full of sins and that was why all this suffering came upon him. But we must also see the positive side of their friendship. They suffered with Job's suffering and decided to accompany him. They did not abandon him. What happened was that the situation that Job was going through was beyond his understanding. Sometimes we make the mistake of giving advice to people in the church about things that we don't know about and that if we went through them, we would possibly act in the same way.

I remember a simpler situation once when my wife and I were spiritually counselling a couple with a child. We suggested that the mother take their son to bed early. In theory, we knew what needed to be done, but we did not understand the sacrifice and how to deal with a child his age. Later, when we had our girls, it was when we realised how difficult it was to always put that into practice. Well, if you look at this example, you realise how simple any analogy can be when compared to Job's suffering. Sorry, but I can't find anything that comes close. Job's suffering is big league.

Unfortunately, Job's friends lacked much wisdom in providing comfort, even though they wanted to. The scriptures say that *"Some people make cutting remarks, but the words of the wise bring healing."* (Proverbs 12:18). If Job's friends were wise, they should bring relief with their words and no more pain. Their words were really cruel in such a situation. This added more emotional suffering to Job.

I have been through situations a bit similar to that in my life as a Christian. I have been in situations where supposedly spiritual people have focused on making me see the biblical part that I have to see when going through a difficult situation. They do not consider for a single moment the emotional part of what I am experiencing. My friend Jesús Cruz, was someone who, in moments of my anxiety as a baby Christian in Puerto Rico, was able to relate to my emotions and to go deeply into my heart. And it wasn't that he overlooked my sin. When he had to challenge me, he challenged me to repent.

With Job's suffering, we can also see that not only personal sin leads to difficult situations in our walk with God, but we see that when there is sin involved, it must be eliminated and it must be overcome. Job suffered because Satan wanted to go his way to punish him. He wanted to cause suffering and destruction. Job's example should teach us to have more convictions

Job's example should serve us to have more convictions about our perseverance.

about our perseverance. He was a man like you and me. The difference was his heart and his commitment to God. Any of us can do the same and much more if we always stick to God's teachings.

I am almost certain that Job did not expect a reward from God. It is possible that at one point he had lost all hope. However, because of his faithfulness and his convictions, he became a great instrument of God to give us great spiritual lessons. Job endured through suffering and, like Jesus, God exalted him to a level he never imagined. In the end, God restored his material prosperity, gave him more sons and daughters, and gave him years of life to enjoy. Job's daughters were the most beautiful in the world and his wealth was greater than before (Job 42:12-17). Job proved what the prophet Joel says that God rewards us for the years of suffering and destruction (Joel 2:25-

27). But for that you have to persevere. Job really persevered in his walk with God despite the suffering.

Let us learn the lessons of Job's suffering. Let us look inside our hearts to make sure that we are clean and that when we suffer, it is not because of our sins, but because we do what pleases God. Let's suffer with a good attitude and trust our God. Let's not hold any bitterness in our hearts despite the reactions we see in the people around us. Let's persevere in our walk with God, and he will give us a great reward.

TO REFLECT

1. Personally, to what extent are you willing to suffer to remain faithful to God?

2. If you were in Job's shoes, would you resist that suffering? And don't tell me that people did not wear shoes at that time.

3. How much material possession are you willing to let God take from you and still remain faithful?

4. What health loss situation can you withstand and still persevere in your walk with God?

IV

Daniel: A Fireproof Man

"Those who are wise will shine as bright as the sky, and those who lead many to righteousness will shine like the stars forever."

- *DANIEL 12:3*

Daniel, a man of deep convictions for God, had to go through dark valleys of suffering and not only he stayed faithful but also, with his righteousness, he could help soften the heart of a cruel and idolatrous king. Daniel, along with his other three friends, Hananiah, Mishael, and Azariah, was asked, to please the king, deny his God and worship a golden statue. The convictions of Daniel and his friends were such that they were willing to die rather than deny their God. And they weren't just willing to die, they were willing to die in a fiery furnace. But they did not turn away from God. They persevered and received their reward.

Does this remind you of any other story? Does this look like Jesus? What would you have done in this case? Personally, I don't think I would have resisted. And I hope my answer doesn't discourage you from continuing to read this book. This isn't really about me. I am simply writing about these men and I would like to imitate them. Well, or maybe it demotivates you too if I tell you that I would have done the same. If I tell you that, I'm possibly doing it to show you what I am not and to try to look like Superman. Sometimes situations arise in our lives and we are not sure how we would react. But I am sure that when we sincerely and wholeheartedly love God, we understand the basic principles of staying faithful and we live gratefully for what Jesus did for us; there is no situation, no matter how difficult it is, that we cannot courageously face. I hope that we never have to face situations like this in our lives. In case they are presented to us today, they are opportunities for us to show our convictions for our God.

But who really was Daniel and what lessons can we learn from this super man? Excuse me, a super man or an ordinary man with convictions for his God? I can say both. An ordinary man with deep convictions for his God can become more than a super man. Let's start by saying that Daniel was just a young man exiled from Jerusalem to Babylon. He was taken to Babylon when the king of Judah, Jehoiakim, was captured by Nebuchadnezzar (Daniel 1:1-2). A special characteristic that we can see in Daniel is that he was from a royal family, distinguished, cultured, and intelligent. Today we look at these characteristics and from all perspectives that I look at, it occurs to me that it would be a real challenge for someone like him to be a man of God with deep convictions, who is willing to give his life to remain faithful and to focus on helping others.

The convictions of Daniel and his friends were such that they were willing to die rather than deny their God.

Sometimes our lack of conviction, our weaknesses, and our stereotypes lead us to reach people like ourselves. And sometimes we want to reach people that we don't feel challenged by them. For example, if we are professionals with a degree, it is easier for us to reach students of non-professionals. We believe that people with Daniel's characteristics would not even come to church to seek God. But looking at Daniel's example, we must understand that God calls all kinds of people. We could see someone not so good looking to our eyes and could become a person of great convictions for God. It is not what our human eyes can see, but what God sees in the hearts of people.

In the case of Daniel, strengths were why he was chosen for training and to begin his service in the king's palace. Since the beginning, Daniel and his friends showed their convictions. They decided not to contaminate themselves with the king's food, which was considered to be special and for special people (Daniel 1:8-9). Their convictions led God to bless them abundantly (Daniel 1:17-21).

Because of the wisdom that God gave Daniel, he was able to help the king when the king was facing a difficult situation. Daniel interpreted the dream for him, and it was a great relief. Because of his wisdom, the king placed Daniel and, at Daniel's request also his friends, in high positions in the administration of the province of Babylon (Daniel 2:48-49). Furthermore, because of what Daniel did, the king was able, at least verbally, to recognize the greatness of God and to worship him (Daniel 1:47).

What can you normally expect from people holding public office? All this is a sign of corruption. We can see the different examples today and historically in our countries. Daniel and his friends, on the other hand, are a great example of righteousness and faithfulness to God.

What can we expect of people around them, seeing the convictions of these men and the positions they are holding to support the king? The same thing has always happened: envy and rivalries. From those times to the present, we see how envious people are and all the pressure that is put on righteous people and, especially, on people with deep convictions for God.

Daniel's colleagues were jealous and envious with his success.

From this point on, I will describe what these men went through and how their convictions for God, despite the difficulties, made an eternal impact on people at that time and on us today. You can also see what awaits at the end for people who are against children of God who persevere.

Daniel and his friends continued to excel in everything they did for the king and they did not lose their convictions to God. Therefore, they had a great impact on the administration and God blessed them. But, as normally happens in this world and the Bible clearly says, a person's success provokes envy (Ecclesiastes 4:4). Daniel's colleagues were jealous and envious of their success. That is why they sought a way to throw a shadow on Daniel and his friends before the king. But, as I have mentioned above, external attacks do not harm people. What destroys is what is in the heart. The bitterness of those people ultimately contributed to the impact that Daniel and his friends had. Those people, on the other hand, were destroyed.

It looks like Daniel had a great influence on his friends and, possibly, his friends on him as well. The Bible does not mention it directly, but we see the results of their convictions. Those people, using their worldly intelligence, sought to create a situation that would not fail to slander Daniel's friends. And from the world's point of view, it didn't fail. But God never abandons his children. God always accompanies us in the most difficult moments when we are faithful to him. Daniel's friends were willing to be thrown into the fiery furnace because they did not worship the golden statue and for keeping their convictions toward their God, our God (Daniel 3).

Daniel and his friends were sure that, one way or another, God was going to help them. They were willing to keep their convictions, even if God did not help them in that situation. Their convictions were so deep that nothing made them change. Instead, all the king's supporters went like cows to the slaughterhouse to worship the golden statue. They sought to please a man regardless, although he was acting against God. We continue to see this today. Many people think that a politician or any person of influence is the solution to our problems.

God acted powerfully on this occasion and saved these three people from the flames of a burning furnace. This made quite an impact on the king and, I'm sure, on other people around him as well. Again, the convictions of these men led King Nebuchadnezzar to praise God when he said: *"Praise be to the God of Shadrach, Meshach and Abednego, who has sent his angel and rescued his servants! They trusted in him and defied the king's command and were willing to give up their lives rather than serve or worship any god except their own God."* (Daniel 3:28). If we analyse it closely, God is using these situations to shape the king's heart. And what happened to those who slandered them? They paid the price of those who are dragged away by their own evil desires, they died (James 1:14-15). They were finally thrown into the fiery furnace (Daniel 3.22-23).

But just as Satan does not rest and always prowls around like a roaring lion looking for someone to devour (1 Peter 5:8), envy and jealousy continue to be Satan's instruments. Daniel continued to help the king (Daniel 5) and stood out over the other supervisors because of his great ability, skills, and convictions (Daniel 6:3). But the other governors looked for a reason to accuse him of maladministration. Again, they convinced the king with lies to issue a decree affecting Daniel directly. This time again, Daniel was willing to pay the price of staying faithful to God.

The decree was that for thirty days anyone who prays to any god or human being, except the king, shall be thrown into the lions' den (Daniel 6:7). They knew, knowing Daniel's righteousness and his love for his God, that he would not obey the decree. Again, they convinced the king thinking they could destroy a man of God. They had Daniel thrown into the lions' den. Do you want me to continue describing what happened? No, I'm pretty sure we've all heard the story. Since God never abandons his faithful followers, he sent an angel to protect Daniel and the lions caused no harm to him.

What would you do if you found yourself in a situation like that? Would you have had the faith to trust that you would survive? If you say yes, please lend a little bit of your faith to me because I don't have it. Daniel was spared from death and being eaten by lions, and he was given a higher position in the administration. His accusers, on the other hand, were thrown into the lions' den, along with their relatives, and they were torn to pieces before reaching the bottom.

> *Daniel was willing to pay the Price of staying faithful to God.*

Knowing the history, would you dare to raise slander like this to someone who trusts God?

Please, do not do anything in your life in favour of God if you do not want to. But don't you ever slander a child of God in your life. You will reap what you sow.

I have faced situations of envy in my professional life but none compares to this one. Insecure and mediocre people in the work environment, since they don't have a way to stand out on their own merits, normally seek to tarnish others. If they tarnish them, the little they do momentarily will look to shine. When similar situations have happened to me, God has always taken me to unimagined positions and has blessed me more than I had expected.

When you work in an environment with good professionals and people of good character, those things that I mention are lessened but it does not mean that they are completely eliminated. Even in the kingdom, there are quarrels and envy with which you have to deal with to avoid division and destruction.

In my first job as a professional working for the university, the situation was challenging due to the lack of resources. But there was a good atmosphere and fellowship. My first real challenge came when I quit that job and moved to Santo Domingo to work as a sales supervisor for two plastics companies that were run together.

The environment was very hostile. First, I had to share my supervisory role with someone older than me, with experience working in the Dominican public sector and with less academic preparation. The first thing I saw was how this person affected another one who was going to hold his position. This person was an assistant to the marketing consultant. Possibly, his expectation was to be promoted to be a sales supervisor. When he saw these two other people arrive at the office, he may have felt envy. I saw how this person tried to demotivate us about what we were going to do. And I think his ideas were one of the factors for the other person to give up and quit.

I thought I was going to be the only sales supervisor. The sales manager told me to get ready as we both would take care of everything. Suddenly, I saw that the person I'm referring to was also appointed as a sales supervisor to manage half of the sales force. As a naive young man without malice as a professional and trusting in my academic training. I was not worried. But I didn't know exactly what he was doing to me. What I did know was that the relationship between us was very hostile. The whole work environment in the company was weird.

Well, let me not extend the story. Do you know what happened to me? God took me out of that environment. I felt great joy when two months later they gave me my cancellation letter. That was my starting point to becoming a disciple in Puerto Rico. God had a much better plan for me, but first, he wanted me to learn a little about the world and all its difficulties.

I also had another difficult experience working for another company after being a disciple. My nature has always been to think positively toward people and to try to reflect on what I was learning in the Bible. Most of the experience I had until that point was all my time in the academic environment and my simple life growing up in the countryside of the Dominican Republic. I heard all the gossip about other people. And I felt good that they weren't talking about me. Of course not. They did not speak in front of me. Obviously, if they talked about others, they also talked about me when I wasn't there.

Then God also took me out of that environment. I couldn't explain why I was in that company. I was the sales supervisor for a beverage company. After holding that position, I was for about seven months without a job and, as we say in the Dominican Republic when we cannot supply our needs, "I was feeding myself with air". But God was also shaping my heart for more blessings.

Then I spent a year in an organization with a religious focus where the situation was better. Later, I went to work for eleven years for the Government of the United States of America. There I had sweet and bitter experiences. Again, always with a positive approach, I was focused on doing my job to the best of my abilities.

Obviously, there were always many aspects to improve, including interpersonal relations. I must also confess that at one point I "threw in the towel" and gave up inviting my classmates to church activities. I invited them and they always refused the invitation.

I was disappointed to see people who did not think that someone could tell the truth. They believed that other people were always saying one thing, but meaning another. But the most difficult situation was at the end when I was told in a meeting that the main problem in the office was me. Do you know why? Because I didn't join them in gossiping and lying. I must also confess that sometimes I let myself be dragged down by the group, sharing certain conversations that I shouldn't have to avoid being left out of the group.

Possibly, not being completely radical prevented me from making a bigger impact. Later, when I wasn't planning to get a job, but to work independently, God allowed me to share the work environment with a wonderful team for a little over a year. I think this was a great blessing from God so that I could retire to work independently again with a good taste and attitude towards the work environment in the Dominican Republic. Well, what happened, in that case, was that I met people very similar to the people I originally shared with when I was working at the university, old friends from the academic environment. Today, in 2023, I am working as an employee in the Foreign Service for the Dominican Government. I enjoy my job, but those issues in the work environment continue to be the same or worse. I will continue to be a disciple and do my best to bring my friends to Jesus.

I share my experience with you but I hope you will never think that I want to compare myself with Daniel or his friends. His convictions were so strong that, no matter how radical I am, I think, as John said about Jesus, that the straps of their sandals I am not worthy to untie. We must imitate men of Daniel's convictions to make an impact on other people and persevere in our walk with God. Strive to be fireproof.

TO REFLECT

1. Do you really believe the whole story of Daniel?

2. To what extent would you resist the pressure of others and slander without opening your mouth to defend yourself, trusting that your God will come to your aid?

3. What impact are you making by leading others to shine like the stars?

4. What is your personal definition of conviction and righteousness?

V

Stephen: His Convictions Moved Jesus' Heart

"But Stephen, full of the Holy Spirit, looked up to heaven and saw the glory of God, and Jesus standing at the right hand of God.".

- *ACTS 7:55*

A way to persevere in our walk with God when we are facing difficult times is always thinking about what Jesus would do in that situation. This was a very basic principle learned since my early days as a disciple of Jesus.

Thinking about this and doing what he would do will not free us from suffering, obviously, but it will strengthen us and, in the future, we will receive our deserved crown. Stephen is a great example of someone who sought to imitate Jesus until the end of his days and he became the first martyr for his cause.

For your information, in case you didn't know, Stephen was not one of the twelve apostles. Stephen was one of those chosen when the church began to grow and administrative problems began to arise regarding the daily distribution for Greek-speaking and Hebrew-speaking widows (Acts 6:1-5). For your information, I had to refresh my memory and review while writing this book. This was not something fresh in my mind. When I started to write, I thought I was writing about one of the twelve apostles. Stephen did not walk with Jesus. He doesn't appear on stage before.

> *Stephen is a great example of someone who sought to imitate Jesus until the end of his days, becoming the first martyr for his cause.*

Stephen was chosen after many prayers from the apostles so that God would enlighten them. The apostles were looking for people they could trust, had good understand, and were filled with the Holy Spirit. He had all those characteristics. But the fact that God enlightened the apostles to choose these people was not a guarantee that everyone would stay focused on doing what they had to do or maintaining their convictions. This is similar to what Jesus did when he chose his apostles. For example, within the group was Judas Iscariot.

Within this group for administration purposes, there was also Nicolas. I leave you the task of investigating who Nicolas was, and what happened to him or his followers later. Then you can share the results with me in return for writing this book for you. To give you a clue, look for the Nicolaitans. But I let you know that the action of the Nicolaitans is mentioned, but not Nicolas's. As it has happened with different religious movements, it is possible that after the death of the leader, some wanted to distort Nicholas' teachings. But don't get off track, Wagner, please continue to focus on Stephen, some of you may say.

Possibly what was expected from Stephen was just to be a good administrator. It was not necessarily expected to give the spiritual testimony he gave. But it happens to be that a person who understands what his responsibility of walking at the feet of Jesus means does not separate between what is a normal life and life in the church. The focus is to please God always. Stephen always spoke guided by the Holy Spirit. And this really bothered other non-spiritual people (Acts 6:8-10). Be-

> *Stephen always spoke guided by the Holy Spirit.*

cause of this, and because they couldn't face or beat a spiritual person, they lied about Stephen to try to beat him.

I have mentioned it before and I repeat it. What people do or say doesn't harm me regardless of how scary it may look. What harms me is what comes out of my heart. None of the slanders against Stephen hurt him, although they did make him suffer. On the other hand, these slanders increased his convictions and set the stage for Christianity to make the impact we have seen. When Stephen was arrested and brought before the Sanhedrin, they gave him the opportunity to testify before the authorities. They saw his conviction and also his innocence as they saw his face like an angel.

Like Jesus, when he was accused, Stephen did not defend himself. He gave a powerful testimony of Jesus by preaching his word. Stephen always based his testimony on the Scriptures. He talked from Abraham to Jesus and never lowered his convictions to defend his life. To persevere in our walk with God, we must stick to the Scriptures and always use them to testify. Rather than using our own ideas, we must use the Scriptures. We must witness about a crucified Jesus and always focus on shaping the hearts of people to come to Jesus.

> *Stephen always based his testimony on Scriptures.*

If we reflect on Stephen's defence, we see that people listened to him. With God's help, he was able to give the testimony he had to give. And it looks like he was able to do it without interruptions.

Difficult situations in our lives, as in Stephen's, lead us to other good situations and places where we didn't imagine we could go. What is the most difficult situation that you think you could face? Go to jail? Get kidnaped? Death? They would be difficult situations for me at this time. It would be embarrassing and challenging. But if I have to face them because of my convictions for Christ, I try to prepare myself to face them with joy and to carry the message of Jesus. I know it's easy to say and hard to face reality. But the cross of Jesus and all these testimonies must shape my heart to face any situation that arises in my walking with God.

Stephen could have been disappointed giving such a good testimony as he did and not seeing people changing. Instead of changing, people got angrier. Still, he didn't give up. He kept his same spiritual focus. He was confident that his perseverance would bear fruit sooner or later. His perseverance was part of the basis for Paul's future convictions. Paul witnessed his stoning and his death and gave his approval.

While they stoned Stephen and while he was about to die in such a cruel way, he did not focus on his situation. Like Jesus, Stephen did not hold any resentment against those who killed him. Instead, he asked God to forgive them because they did not know what they were doing (Acts 7:60). In addition to Paul, it is very likely that others who were there when Stephen was stoned are also in heaven with him. Maybe other people also changed their lives because of his great testimony and his convictions.

> *Like Jesus, Stephen did not hold any resentment against those who killed him.*

Stephen persevered in his walk with God to the very end. With his perseverance, he was able to glorify God and move Jesus' heart in heaven. When Jesus is mentioned in heaven next to God, he is usually seated. In this particular situation, when Stephen saw him, Jesus was standing up at the right-hand side of God. I can imagine what Jesus was saying at that moment. "Well done my faithful and righteous servant. You have persevered. Come, take your deserved place with us". Hopefully, this can also be said of each one of us when we persevere in our walk with God. Do our convictions move Jesus' heart?

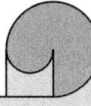

TO REFLECT

1. Which of your actions in life do you think have moved Jesus' heart?

2. Would you resist being stoned for remaining faithful to Jesus? I said stoned. The stones are hard. Without anaesthetics.

3. Have you gone through situations of real suffering for being a Christian, or are you willing to suffer to be one?

4. Have you complained about simple insignificant suffering?

VI

Abraham: An Unshakeable Faith

"…..and all peoples on earth will be blessed through you.".

- *GENESIS 12:3*b

Wagner, do you think you can make any contribution by talking about Abraham? You must understand that Abraham is someone so well known that whatever you write will be just repetition. Wow! It is true. But no.

The fact that someone thinks this way does not mean that they would be thinking differently from me. I thought about it a lot and was about to delete Abraham from the list of biblical examples to include in this part of the book. Then I thought and decided to include him. I thought that although many people have written about Abraham, his testimony is too great and I could not leave it out. In addition, sometimes we think that we cannot make a new contribution and that people will not be inspired by what we write. Then we get the feedback on the impact of that and we are surprised.

This is especially the case with people who come after us. From our experience we believe that our ideas are very simple and then we see the impact that they have on young people. Sometimes ideas come to us because God wants us to share them. Let's wait until the end to see what we can learn from his example

Why Abraham and not one of his ancestors or one of his ancestors after Noah, like his father Terah or one of his brothers or his grandfather Nahor, son of Shem, who was the son of Noah? Well, we also see here that Abraham was the great-grandson of Shem and the great-great-grandson of Noah. And was that God in that period of time and generations did not find someone like him? Judging from the blessings to his direct ancestors, I understand that the blessings to Abraham and his offspring were also blessings to his father, his grandfather, and everyone else down to Noah. I don't think it's that God hasn't seen the hearts of others or that others haven't had a heart for God. It was that Abraham had an extraordinary heart. God didn't need a good heart; he needed a super heart to set a super foundation for the future.

> *Opportunities to make an impact for the glory and honour of God still exist.*

The work is not over yet. God continues to search for those hearts. Opportunities to make an impact for the glory and honour of God still exist. Or do you think the opportunities have already passed? Definitely not. God continues to work to recover his children. The way God is going to bring the most people to him is through people who have a super heart. Are you simply looking to persevere? Well, persevering in your walk with God is the goal, but to make sure that we persevere, we have to give our best for God.

> *God keeps his promises today, but many people, do not accept them*

We cannot expect little when we know that God can give us more. Someone once said "think big and you will fly, think small and you will fall". We must seek to make the greatest possible impact on God and not simply persevere.

Abraham was a man of faith. We have seen the impact of it throughout history, in our days and we will continue to see it for eternity. Where does Abraham's impact lie? Basically, in his faith and his deep convictions for his God, our God. We see his faith, but we also see his heart, his obedience, and the actions that accompany that faith.

Abraham was focused on always doing God's will and not his own will. This is described when he let Lot decide which part of the land he wanted to go to and he would accept whatever Lot left him (Genesis 13). But before that, we must describe Abraham's call to leave his father's house at the age of 75 for an unknown land. God promised to make Abraham a great nation, bless him and make him famous. All this is described in the Bible from Genesis 12 to 25.

Let's reflect a little on this. Who for convenience does not decide to make a decision in one way or another? I consider that it is not difficult for a person to make a decision when what awaits him are great blessings and fame. That's true. But in Abraham's decision, before all those benefits, what was seen was his faith. Sometimes God promises us those benefits and we don't trust him. Abraham trusted the God's promises.

Throughout the Bible, we see all the promises of God, but we also see many people who do not trust. God keeps his promises today and many people do not accept them. Are you trusting all the promises that God makes to you when you are obedient to him? God makes the same promises to us that he made to Abraham. God does not overlook the obedience and faith of his children. I dare to make a radical statement. Even today God can start another journey in the world with someone who has the faith, heart, and determination of Abraham. Do you believe it? God is the same today as he has always been. Faithlessness and wickedness abound in the world today. The temptation to sin is very great and God rejoices to see people who love him and are willing to make any sacrifice for him and to serve his people.

The fact that Abraham obeyed and trusted God with his promises does not mean that he was not going to encounter difficulties. God's promises are always fulfiled, but along the way, we have to continue to maintain our faith to overcome all the obstacles that come our way. Abraham may have become discouraged along the way when a severe food shortage arose while he was living in the Negev region. He had to go to live in Egypt for some time (Genesis 12:10). Notice that Abraham did not return to Haran from where he had come. He continued his journey. Sometimes we go through situations in our lives and what we do is look back. We try to go back, but God wants us to always look forward.

With the situation of lack of food, Abraham was not discouraged. He continued to trust in the promises of the Lord and persevered. Furthermore, by going to Egypt, he took the risk of being killed because of the beauty of his wife, but God protected him. Again, we see an episode here, or we can say it was the first, where someone leaves a place due to lack of food and then has to return. But at least because of Sarah (Sarai), Abraham received some gifts from Pharaoh and became very rich.

According to the Scriptures, Abraham was also a brave warrior (Genesis 14). When Lot was taken prisoner, Abraham was the one who rescued him by defeating four kings. These four kings had previously defeated five others. Abraham defeated them with only the help of his servants. Presumably all the training the servants had was from Abraham as their leader. Furthermore, Abraham was not focused on getting rich off someone else's possessions. His focus was only to do the will of God. This caused the priest Melchizedek to also bless him when he said to him: *"Blessed be Abram by God Most High, Creator of heaven and earth. And praise be to God Most High, who delivered your enemies into your hand."* (Genesis 14:19-20).

> *...with God's help we can overcome any obstacle and persevere in our walk with him.*

It is also clearly seen that Abraham did not defeat the kings by himself. He beat them because God caused him to beat them. This shows us that with God's help we can overcome any obstacle and persevere in our walk with him.

Later, God makes a covenant with Abraham. (Genesis 15). God promises that his reward will be very great. Abraham considered that blessings and rewards were worthless if, in the end, his heir was to be one of his servants. But God promised him that his heir would be his own son and not a stranger. God also promised him that the number of his descendants would be like the stars in the sky that cannot be counted. Well, not just one son, but countless generations would come from him. *"Abram believed the Lord, and he credited it to him as righteousness."* (Genesis 15:6).

Would you have believed all these promises? God's promises are kept today for those who are faithful to him. Do you believe it? What do you think God is not capable of doing in your life? God is a God of the impossible according to the eyes or the human mind.

With God's promises, we also need to be willing to accept all the challenges that they bring. God warned Abraham that his descendants were going to live in a foreign country, that they would be slaves, and that they would also be mistreated for four-hundred years. But he also promised him that they would later walk out free and with great possessions. (Genesis 15:13-14). This sounds a lot like God's promise to us in Mark 10:29-30, that we will receive a hundred times what we leave for the kingdom of God, but with persecutions. To receive all these blessings, we need to trust God, be willing to suffer for his sake, and persevere in our walk with him.

Since God promised Abraham a son, Abraham could have been satisfied and could have seen his promise fulfilled when God gave him Ishmael, the son of the slave Hagar. However, God still had a greater blessing for him. It is possible that his blessing would be cut short if it was not also shared with his wife Sara. Therefore, God, seeing Abraham's heart, promised him that he would have a son born to his wife when they were old and Sarah was past the age of childbearing (Genesis 18). That promise was fulfiled with the birth of Isaac (Genesis 21:3). Isaac was born when Abraham was one hundred years old (Genesis 21:5).

At every moment, the heart of Abraham is seen. His approach was also always to serve and not to be served. In the episode when the angels appeared to him, his focus was on serving them (Genesis 18:4-8). God blesses those hearts. We see it clearly in Jesus, but that comes from the beginning.

But what crowned Abraham as the father of faith was his obedience to God when he asked him to sacrifice his son Isaac. After God had given Abraham his son Ishmael, as a result of his union with the slave of his wife Sarah, God granted his wife to give him a son as well. This was a great blessing for the marriage. And for whom was the blessing itself, for Sarah or for Abraham? The original promise was to Abraham, but the blessing came through his wife. They both enjoyed the blessing. This resembles Hannah's blessing of having Samuel after she was barren and begged God to give her a son. Both Hannah and her husband Elkanah enjoyed the blessing. But the blessing itself came through Hannah's prayers (1 Samuel 1:15-16).

After God gave Abraham his son Isaac, he asked him to offer him as a sacrifice. Abraham obeyed God and did not waver. He walked several days to the place where he was going to sacrifice him and it is not seen that at any time he hesitated to do so.

Something shocking about Abraham was also that he asked those who accompanied him to stay while he went to offer the burnt offering with his son and then the two would return. We can wonder in this case if Abraham was actually saying that the two of them would return or was it a way to avoid being asked some question in which he would be at a crossroads to reveal his plan. Knowing Abraham's faith, we can infer that it is possible that Abraham was trusting that God had the power to even resurrect Isaac after he was offered as a sacrifice.

Abraham obeyed God and did not hesitate.

Let's think for a moment about what could happen to Abraham emotionally and what could happen to any of us in a similar situation. Isaac tells Abraham "Father…we have the wood and the fire, but where is the lamb for the burnt offering? (Genesis 22:7). In today's parlance we might have a child say something like "daddy or lovely dear daddy." How would you feel having your son calling you daddy and you knowing what you are going to do with him? Would you continue with your plans? Well, again, if you say yes, I'm asking for a little of borrowed faith. Abraham overcame his emotions and continued with his plan out of obedience to God.

As God promises, when we are faithful to him, he blesses all our generations.

Finally, God saw his heart to obey him to the end. Since God saw his heart, he did not allow him to harm the boy. For Abraham, it was as if God had returned his child to him. I imagine Abraham taking a deep breath at that moment. Isaac's obedience must also be highlighted. The Bible does not describe Isaac's reaction, but we can infer that he had to be very obedient to allow himself to be tied up and about to be sacrificed.

It is very likely that, as a father, Abraham prepared Isaac in advance during his life to also be an obedient person to God and very submissive. It is not for nothing that we then also see all the blessings that God gives to Isaac as if he were Abraham himself. We can even say that Isaac's life was easier than his father's because of the foundation that Abraham had already prepared. As God promises, when we are faithful to him, God blesses our generations (Exodus 20:4-6).

Like Abraham, God allows us to go through difficult situations until we reach the limit to see if we resist and persevere in our walk with him to the end. Jesus did. Abraham did. Stephen did. And many others. Ruth Espinal did. José Flores did. Damian Jean-Baptist did. Will you? Will you face all the obstacles of this life and persevere? We must imitate the example of our ancestors and persevere in our walk with God and have an unbreakable faith.

TO REFLECT

1. Do you truly know Abraham's story of faith and its impact?

2. Where would you be willing to go if God calls you?

3. What would you be willing to give if God asked you to give?

4. Which "Isaac" are you willing to sacrifice for God?

VII

Joseph: An Unconditional Love for God

"....How then could I do such a wicked thing and sin against God??"

- *GENESIS 39:9b.*

I have heard many examples of people facing difficult situations in their walk with God. I relate to some of them. They help me strengthen my convictions to obey God and remain faithful. Some of those examples are challenging. But seeing the sacrifice of Jesus on the cross, I trust that I can go through the same situation and overcome the obstacles. However, when it comes to emotional challenges and temptations and looking at things spiritually, I believe that Joseph's situation was tougher than any other.

Joseph is a good example of a young man who was able to resist sexual temptation.

Once I heard an expression in Spanish that translated means that a sheet of paper accepts anything we write on it about what we can do and how much we can bear a difficult situation. However, when we face reality is when we see how strong we are actually. I always think that a good starting point to persevering in our walk with God is to be totally convinced that we will stay faithful regardless of the circumstances.

Joseph's story is presented in the Bible from Genesis 37 to 50. It is a very interesting one. It is a great story of perseverance and faith. He was hated by his brothers, he was sold as a slave, he was slandered, and some people were not grateful to him when he expected. All that happened was to push him to lose his faith. However, those situations and his faith were used by God to make him an eternal icon and hero.

The case of Joseph, his love for God, his firmness to pay bad with good, and to overcome sexual temptation is something to motivate us all. Currently, temptations and sexual sins are one of the main causes for many people to abandon God after making a commitment to follow him. It looks like these temptations are everywhere. The whole society is leading to fill our minds with all this garbage. I'm not just talking about sex but about the wrong interpretation of what sex means. The media is seeking to distort the right view in our minds. And Satan is very aware of that to use it as one of his fighting weapons. He knows that this is a weakness for many people. But those who focus on Jesus and on always pleasing God can overcome any temptation.

Joseph is a good example of a young man who was able to resist sexual temptation. He was willing to pay a high price, even beyond his expectation, to remain faithful to God. To enjoy a temporary pleasure without considering immediate and future consequences can lead a person to fall into this type of sin. And it is much more tempting to do so when avoiding it leads us to a huge emotional sacrifice and punishment when slander is raised against us.

Today, a person like Joseph would possibly have his manhood questioned. Joseph's love for God enabled him to endure slander and imprisonment. God knew why he chose him over all his brothers.

> *Joseph's love for God enabled him to endure slander and imprisonment.*

Joseph was chosen by God over his brothers for a great mission. God chose him to save his family from starving. This, however, did not mean that he did not have to face challenging situations. God knew which diamond he was choosing to polish. God is wise and does not waste time using low-quality materials. When God wants to refine us by fire, he does not want to waste his time to get a final result that is bad.

Possibly, other people did not see the heart of Joseph. God, who does not pay attention to appearances, but to the heart, as the Scriptures say, knew what he had in hand. Since he was a child, Joseph understood that God had great plans for him. Understanding this was the basis for his confidence, despite the sufferings.

Joseph had an unconditional love for God. He was the result of his father Jacob's love for Rachel, for which he was willing to work for seven years with his uncle Laban. He had to work seven more years because he did not receive her as promised. In addition, as in many of the cases in which God wants to do great things in a person's life, the usual drama was present. Joseph was about not to be born.

In addition to all the other bad things that some of Joseph's brothers did, you can also see the wickedness in their hearts and their misbehaviour. In Genesis 37: 2 we see how Joseph went against the grain facing the wickedness of his brothers and bringing the complaint of their wickedness to his father Jacob. This is very similar to what I have described about Noah in Chapter 17, suggesting that he also went against the grain.

> *Joseph had an unconditional love for God.*

It is very common today to see people who cover up the misbehaviour of others. Some people do it out of fear of what others may say. Others do it because of their lack of convictions and their weak character. Covering up other people's wickedness occurs even in churches. We see people in sin and we don't confront them. These people include pastors and leaders. Some pastors and leaders live in sin and they don't confront visible sins or go deep into the hearts of their members.

Joseph did not tolerate sin in his life. Neither did he tolerate sin in his brothers'. Just like it happens today, it was obvious the wicked would not tolerate a righteous person. As Proverbs 29:27 says, *"The righteous detest*

> *Joseph did not tolerate sin in his life. Neither did he tolerate sin in his brothers'.*

the dishonest; the wicked detest the upright." Does this sound like any current situation?

The problem was also worsened by his father Jacob's favouritism. This favouritism made his brothers hate him more and not even greet him (Genesis 37:4). The good thing is that God always allows situations to happen with a purpose. He uses any situation to teach and train us. With the family situation in Joseph's house, we learn great lessons about what not to do with our children and how to help them.

> *"The righteous detest the dishonest; the wicked detest the upright."*
> -Proverbs 29:27

We must keep in mind how God blesses righteous people beyond expectation. Joseph was righteous despite living with brothers who were not. Since he was young, God revealed in a dream the great plans he had for him (Genesis 37:5-11). I don't think it was that Joseph decided to be faithful to God because he knew that God was going to bless him. I think it was the opposite. God was going to bless Joseph for his righteousness and his love for him.

God's paradoxical way of working began when Joseph's brothers decided to trade him as a slave to the Ishmaelites, who were on their way to Egypt. Neither Joseph nor anyone else imagined what God was preparing in his life. His brothers thought they were harming him. However, with his wickedness, they were helping to fulfil God's will for Joseph and for his people. God really makes his plans come true above all else even if people oppose them. God can use even stones or non-living objects to do his work (Matthew 3:9).

Joseph was upright and faced the sin of his brothers. Unlike Joseph, his brothers sank into sin. And whatever the sin is, that same sin leads to more sin. The first thing his brothers did when they saw Joseph arrive to find out how they were doing was to plan to kill him. In the end, they didn't kill him. They put him in a dry well and then sold him to the Ishmaelites. And the question was how were they going to justify what they did to their father.

> *Sin, as it was not faced and removed with repentance, did the natural thing; it led to more sin.*

Sin, as it was not faced and removed with repentance, did the natural thing; it led to more sin. To hide what they did, they had to lie to their father sending him Joseph's bloodstained coat to make him think that a wild animal had eaten him (Genesis 37:33). And sin continued to bear more sin. These people were cruel to their father causing him pain and not caring about him.

We can also see how not being righteous and not acting at the right time to please God can cause us to miss the opportunity to have an impact. Both Reuben and Judah had ideas to protect Joseph. However, they were not radical nor did they act. By not acting immediately, they missed the opportunity. Later, they found out the other brothers had already sold Joseph to the Ishmaelites.

> *Some opportunities God gives us may be unique and exclusive to us*

Possibly, God gives us unique opportunities to act and to have an impact and we reject them. There may be ideas that come to us or opportunities that come our way that are unique or exclusive. Let's think of several biblical situations that would not have caused an eternal impact if people did not take advantage of them.

If Abraham had not obeyed God, if he had allowed Isaac to marry a Canaanite; and right here, if Joseph had withstood his brothers, who might have killed him; if Joseph had allowed himself to be convinced by Potiphar's wife; if Jesus had called the twelve armies of angels; if Paul had resisted Jesus and continued with his plans to kill the Christians, if I had not been determined to go to Puerto Rico and become a disciple; if you had not become a Christian, assuming that if you are reading this book it is because you are already a believer; if you had not taken the opportunity to invite that friend to church, who has decided to follow Jesus. Well, history could be different. Some opportunities God gives us may be unique and exclusive.

> *Satan disguises himself as any situation, male or female, to try to distract and destroy us.*

Joseph was sold as a slave and God never abandoned him. God does not abandon someone with a surrendered heart like Joseph's.

What his brothers did, which was something external to his heart, did not harm him. On the contrary, it did him good and it was the beginning of the fulfilment of the visions he had. Joseph was sold to Potiphar, Pharaoh's official and captain of his guard (Genesis 37:36). God continued to be with Joseph and to bless him and his Egyptian master. His master made him his personal assistant and steward of his house (Genesis 39:1-6).

Satan never stops doing his job. He can walk away, but only for a while (Luke 4:13). Satan disguises himself to try to distract and destroy us. I imagine that Satan, seeing Joseph's previous convictions and his righteousness when facing so many challenging situations, thought that this tactic to destroy him was going to be infallible and was sure it was going to make Joseph fall.

Satan used Potiphar's wife to tempt Joseph by asking him to sleep with her. Accepting a request like that, from the world's point of view, would have saved Joseph a lot of suffering and, possibly, people could think that no one was going to know about it. Satan probably thought that a good-looking young man would not let this opportunity escape to show his pride and share what a conqueror he was by being with the wife of his master, an official of Pharaoh. However, while men of the world may see a person like her as a great woman, a man of God sees her as exactly what she was, a great piece of trash and social scum.

> *For a man or woman of God there is no price that can buy his convictions.*

Joseph responded to Potiphar's wife's request with deep conviction, as a great man of God does. He replied: *"'With me in charge,' he told her, 'my master does not concern himself with anything in the house; everything he owns he has entrusted to my care. No one is greater in this house than I am. My master has withheld nothing from me except you, because you are his wife. How then could I do such a wicked thing and sin against God?"* (Genesis 39:8-9). And acting as Satan himself, the woman did not stop insisting every day. Possibly Satan thought that the third or fourth or fifth time would be the one. But for a man or woman of God there is no price that can buy his convictions. The only focus of a man or woman of God must be to persevere to the end and be willing to lay down his life if necessary to stand firm.

Joseph's convictions caused this woman to slander him. Although the Bible does not say so, possibly, Joseph, because of his convictions, did not defend himself against the accusations, like Jesus did. Possibly he realised that defending himself was not going to help him at all. It was his word against the word of an official's wife. Do you think the husband would believe Joseph? Impossible. Obviously, Potiphar believed his wife. Possibly Potiphar didn't even take a moment to ask Joseph and get a second opinion on the matter. This angered Joseph's master and sent him to jail, where other king's servants were (Genesis 39: 19-20).

> *God never abandons someone with Deep convictions for him*

Under normal circumstances, this would be the end of Joseph. However, God did not abandon him. God never abandons someone with deep convictions for him. God continued to bless Joseph in prison beyond what he could have imagined and strengthened the foundation for everything we know today about Joseph, his family, and his descendants.

By the blessings of God, Joseph earned the sympathy of the head of the prison. He appointed him as the head of other prisoners (Genesis 39:22). While in jail, God also gave Joseph wisdom to interpret dreams. This wisdom, although people were ungrateful to him, helped him to go out later to interpret Pharaoh's dream.

> *Joseph was also patient in accepting God's will.*

Joseph's humility is also seen in not taking credit for what he did. He understood that the credit belonged to God, who gave him the wisdom to interpret dreams. Moreover, God himself was the one who gave him the interpretation (Genesis 40:8). The interpretation of this dream was ultimately the springboard for Joseph to become the second most important man in Egypt, after Pharaoh. That also laid the foundation for saving his family, God's chosen people (Genesis 41). This was also the beginning of the fulfilment of God's telling to Abraham that his offspring would live and suffer in a foreign place for four hundred years, but then they would be free.

Joseph was also patient in accepting God's will. Joseph asked the king's cupbearer, whose interpretation of the dream was that he was going to be reinstated in his job, and in fact it was, to remember him and speak to the king so that he would get out of jail. However, the cupbearer did not remember Joseph again (Genesis 40:23).

> *God blessed Joseph's righteousness and his unconditional love for him.*

Joseph continued to fulfil his responsibilities in jail and patiently waited for God's will. Joseph could be bitter, thinking that all this was happening to him because of the wickedness of his brothers and because of the slander of Potiphar's wife. Joseph could have also thought that everything was happening to him because he was upright and for telling his father the evil acts of his brothers.

At that point, he could have changed his mind and decided to act differently. He may have thought that being righteous was not worth it, but instead caused him suffering. He decided to continue being upright and always pleasing his God. God blessed Joseph's righteousness and his unconditional love for him.

Although Joseph was not seeking honour, God was looking for a way to exalt him for his righteousness and love. God let situations to happen for Joseph to serve with the gifts that he gave him. Pharaoh's dream was an opportunity that God provided for Joseph to be useful, to get out of prison, to be exalted, and to be appointed Governor of Egypt. And all this was with the purpose of serving his people.

> *Honouring God always has its reward.*

Before Pharaoh, Joseph didn't seek to take credit for his wisdom; he gave honour to God. Honouring God always has its reward. On the contrary, taking honour for ourselves has its negative consequences. Taking honour for himself, when God commanded Moses to tell the rock to let water flow from it, was the cause for him not to enter the promised land (Numbers 20:12). Joseph interpreted Pharaoh's dreams by acting humbly and wisely at the same time. He allowed himself to be used by God. Joseph counselled the king to protect his people from the food shortages that would come for seven years after seven years of plenty. The king trusted him, and that was salvation for the people of Egypt and for the people of God, the family of Joseph, as well.

Because of his spiritual wisdom, his love of God, his humility, and his love for his people, Joseph was made Governor of Egypt. God gave Joseph honour far beyond what he expected, although it seemed that God was punishing him. All this shows that God allows us to face tough situations to shape us and prepare us to receive and manage blessings.

Today many people, including Christians, seek honour by trying to put God aside and rely more on their own talents. That approach only brings suffering and pain. The search for honour and riches makes our lives miserable. Sometimes we want to serve in the church without having the right focus. We want to do it supposedly to serve our God and the church. However, the real intention is that we do it to feed our pride. We want people to see that we are being used to serve and to try to show off that we have more talent than others. It is not until our hearts are shaped to have the right focus, that God uses us as he wants.

> *God allows us to face tough situations to shape us and prepare us to receive and manage blessings.*

The fact that Joseph was appointed by the king as Governor of Egypt was something unpredictable for any human mind. The most predictable thing was that Joseph would be harshly punished and could even die in jail or go out to continue to be a slave. But God never abandons those who are faithful to him, no matter how dark the situation faced may seem. That is something that should increase our faith and strengthen our convictions.

Joseph was the salvation for the Egyptian people and for his family. He was a great administrator. He focused on serving others and not on serving himself or on being served. His excellence in his job, helped the fulfilment of Proverbs 22:29, which says: *"Do you see someone skilled in their work? They will serve before kings; they will not serve before officials of low rank."* Joseph's convictions for his God, his heart, his sacrifice, and his dedication teach us great lessons to persevere in our walk with God despite facing adversity.

> *Not until our hearts are shaped to have the right focus, will not God use us as he wants.*

I reflect on the insignificant adverse situations that I have had to face and how I have allowed myself to be dominated by them. It challenges me when I compare myself with everything Joseph had to face and how he kept his heart always pure. Many times, I let myself be controlled by my emotions, and take revenge in insignificant situations.

One of the situations that affects me the most is driving in the Dominican Republic, especially when I deal with public transportation drivers. As a Christian, one of my main struggles is that. In those situations, my emotions control me. If I compare this with everything that Joseph faced, it is truly insignificant.

Now let's see Joseph's reaction when he met his brothers when they went to Egypt to get food. How would you have reacted to people who mistreated you, hated you, sold you into slavery, and made your father suffer by lying to him? Again, and I repeat it several times, if you tell me that you would have imitated Joseph's action, I ask you to lend me a little of your faith and a good attitude. We need to make sure that we maintain good attitude when facing tough little situations so that we could deal with bigger ones like those Joseph faced (Song of Songs 2:15).

> *We must take advantage of every difficult situation that comes our way to prepare for the future.*

In our walk with God, we are not exempt from reaching these extremes. A similar situation may arise at any time. If we are not prepared to deal with them, we destroy all the sacrifice made to persevere in our walk with God. We must see these situations and learn the lessons. We must take advantage of every difficult situation that comes our way to prepare for the future.

Joseph's reaction to his brothers showed that his trust was in God. He had no bitterness in his heart for what his brothers had done to him. Joseph clearly understood God's plan for him and why he allowed him to go through all of this "unfair" suffering. Do you understand what God is teaching you today through the situations he allows you to go through?

And I say to myself, how good it is to be able to write about this, and how difficult it is to put it into practice when challenging situations arise. But at least I can say that so far I have overcome all the obstacles that have come my way in my walk with God. I am willing to face with courage and faith everything that I may face in the future regardless of their magnitude and calibre. My expectation is that all what I am writing will also help me strengthen myself every day to persevere in my walk with God and to continue being a living testimony of what I write. God still needs people to witness his power and all the blessings received by those who are faithful to him.

> *A heart like Joseph's really moves God. Let's do the same for his glory and honour.*

Sometimes we believe that the particular situations we face are the most difficult that a person can go through. We think that other people's load is lighter than ours. But all of us have our own challenges. We must deal with them in a spiritual way that pleases God and persevere in our walk with him to ultimately receive our reward. A heart like Joseph's really moves God. Let's do the same for his glory and honour. Without expecting any reward, we can see all the blessings that God will shed on us by persevering in our walk with him. May our love for God motivate us to endure.

TO REFLECT

1. What would your attitude be toward people that you expect to protect you and what they do is to hurt you beyond what they could hurt any enemy?

2. How would you react if the only thing you see ahead of you was suffering and slander against you?

3. Why do you think Joseph remained faithful despite all the adversities?

4. If you were in Joseph's situation at Potiphar's house and you received that temptation, what would you do?

VIII

Isaac: God Blesses Obedience

"…. He bound his son Isaac and laid him on the altar, on top of the wood."

- *GENESIS 22:9b.*

When we look for good examples to follow in the Bible, Abraham becomes a shield that blocks us from getting to Isaac. We don't often consider Isaac as the perfect complement to Abraham. Just like Abraham, he is also a hero. His obedience is worthy of imitation. Without diminishing Abraham, we must also consider Isaac's heroism through his obedience.

When I wrote about Abraham and his faith, I did it after much reflecting about him and after having thought that it was not necessary for me to write more because of all what has been written about him. I thought it was rain it poured but then I found what to focus on. Regarding Isaac, I am writing because I understand that not much has been written about him and he is not a character that many people are inspired to preach about. But his obedience is something worthy of imitating. Through his obedience, he was also a great link in Biblical history and a great foundation for the history of God's people.

God asked Abraham to sacrifice his son Isaac (Genesis 22:2). That was a great challenge for Abraham. How many times do you have to think about it to make the decision to sacrifice your son because, let's say, "God is supposedly asking you to do so"? God knew who he chose for this mission. He took Abraham. Thanks to him that he didn't take me. I hope I don't have to face such a challenging situation in my life before God takes me to dwell with him. It would be something very difficult for me.

We must consider that to show us great examples, God chooses people who have been on the brink of not being born or on the brink of death. Then God does miracles and uses those people powerfully. Isaac is one of those great miracles of the Bible. He was born when his dad and his mom had possibly lost all hope of being parents. At that time, Abraham was already 100 years old (Genesis 18 and 21). Let us also compare with the birth of Jesus by the work of the Holy Spirit and the possibility of him being killed by King Herod when he ordered the killing of all children under the age of two.

Isaac is one of those great miracles of the Bible.

Let's look at Isaac's attitude of obedience in two contexts. The first is this one where he was about to be sacrificed. The second is when his father asks him whom to marry.

Isaac is the fruit of a blessing from God to his parents. I imagine that his parents were not left with a blessing of this nature without telling their son about it. And considering that they did, it's very likely that Isaac embraced the same dream about his future as his parents and God himself had. Therefore, although we do not know at what point Abraham let Isaac know that he was going to be killed, it is to be expected that when Abraham told him, both might have had the same feelings. Both could think that their dream was over or that God was going to fulfil his promise that Abraham was going to be the father of nations in another way.

Well, we can speculate many things. But the reality is that at one point Isaac found out that he was going to be killed. I don't think that with Abraham's righteousness, he was going to bargain with Isaac when he tied him up and put him on top of the altar. Nowhere in the Bible we see Isaac's resistance or disobedience recorded. He accepted God's plan. He joined the plans that God had for his parents and for him. His obedience helped him reap the fruits of it in the future, seeing all that God did with his generations. Through him,

God's blessings were fulfiled to Abraham. We can say that he reaped almost exactly the same fruits as his father.

The other situation of Isaac's obedience, and from which we learn many lessons, is when Abraham asks him not to marry a foreign woman from the land where they were living in Canaan, but to marry someone from his family, from his same lineage (Genesis 24). Abraham sent one of his servants in search of a possible wife from his family for Isaac. This act of obedience complements his blessings and his future.

> *Let's trust God, and we will receive blessings beyond expectations.*

In my particular case, I have had to learn a lot in the church. I come from having a heart inclined to follow my emotions. Later, I learned to accept advice and to leave some of my emotions aside. However, when it came to sentimental matters in relationships to create a family and compromise my future, I said that I never was going to give in to something that went against my emotions.

And do you know what? When the time came, my heart was ready to accept good advice even though I didn't see it emotionally. At that moment, my reaction was to think that it could not be possible that I was right and that all others who considered that Guarina was the right woman for me were wrong. I really trusted God and I received a gift beyond what I was expecting. Let's trust God, and we will receive blessings beyond expectations.

In my mind, I had all the physical and personal characteristics of the person I wanted. Some spiritual characteristics, but most of them were merely worldly desires. One of those aspects was the sports focus. However, Guarina had none of that. I dreamed of someone that we would often be in a tennis court or in a table tennis room, or in a chess room, or in a judo room, or in a baseball stadium, etc. But no. She wasn't interested. However, her spiritual gifts far exceed all my expectations.

I have a lady of steel who challenges me to uphold my spiritual convictions. Although her advice doesn't always make me feel good, she always wants me to stand firm and that is what ultimately matters until we reach heaven. I also tell you that, unexpectedly, we found a sport to play together at almost the same level: scrabble. That has given us great satisfaction and strong competitive matchups sometimes. I have also enjoyed her company on a golf course, a sport that was not on my list when we got married. God is faithful and he gives us much more than we expect when we are obedient to him.

> *Without trust in God, a deviation from our plans can be a disaster.*

Each of us has a defined plan as a person. We have individual plans with goals that we would like to achieve at any cost. Sometimes we consider that these plans are the best for us and we do not want them to change. Without trust in God, a deviation from our plans can be a disaster. Trusting God, if our plans follow another path, we know that his plans are much better.

I particularly had my academic and professional plans more or less defined since 1982 when I moved from my little hometown to study at a technical institute in Santiago de los Caballeros, where God has brought me back when I was writing the Spanish version of this book. My plan was to graduate from high school, go to college, pursue a scholarship to study in the United States, return to the Dominican Republic, possibly get married, and then return to the United States to pursue a Ph.D. As I have written in other books, those plans looked very nice and well defined. But God intervened for good and changed them.

Everything went as planned until I returned from my master's degree in the United States. I believed that the next step of getting married was going to happen. I was planning to get married, but God changed the plan for good. He changed my focus from academics and getting married to spiritual plans so that I would become a disciple of Jesus. Precisely, the same person I thought I would marry was the instrument to bring me to the church to become a disciple in Puerto Rico. From then on, everything is history.

God definitely changed everything and has given me much more than I expected. In addition to allowing me to meet him, he has given me professional excellence beyond what I imagined and a satisfaction that exceeds all limits with what I do for my family and to help many other people come to Christ, including everyone I reach with my spiritual and business writing. This is of much more value than what I would have achieved with my individual plans.

God blessed Isaac with the same blessing he promised to Abraham and he continues to bless us with his example and obedience.

"The Lord appeared to Isaac and said, "Do not go down to Egypt; live in the land where I tell you to live. 3 Stay in this land for a while, and I will be with you and will bless you. For to you and your descendants I will give all these lands and will confirm the oath I swore to your father Abraham. 4 I will make your descendants as numerous as the stars in the sky and will give them all these lands, and through your offspring[a] all nations on earth will be blessed,[b] 5 because Abraham obeyed me and did everything I required of him, keeping my commands, my decrees and my instructions." 6 So Isaac stayed in Gerar." (Genesis 26:2-6).

God will bless your obedience beyond what you can imagine. Obey him and you will reap the fruits in the present and in the future. And in the end, he will give you eternal life.

TO REFLECT

1. How would you react if your father told you that he would sacrifice you following God's instruction?

2. As a Christian, what is your biggest challenge to obey?

3. What have you reaped from your obedience that you can share with others if you haven't shared yet? Do not wait any longer to share it. This may have an impact beyond what is expected.

4. What do you need to sacrifice in obedience to God?

IX

Jonathan: A Great Lesson of Love, Friendship, and Sacrifice for Humanity

" and whoever wants to be first must be your slave –."

- *MATTHEW 20:27*

In the good examples that we see in the Bible, it is likely that David is miles away from Jonathan because of everything David did. The tendency may be to talk about David and how his example has made an impact to this day, as a man with a heart after God's. That's true. But where does that leave Jonathan? Jonathan is a worthy example of love and personal sacrifice in favour of David that we need to imitate today inside and outside the religious environment.

We see this in 1 Samuel 18. It is an example to imitate also in the work environment, where the general approach is to fight freely to seek to stand out above others no matter what that entails. Jonathan was the opposite and is often forgotten. He is highlighted most when it comes to establishing good friendships (1 Samuel 18:1). However, this approach that I describe on love and sacrifice I have not seen in any other writing or preaching.

Jonathan's example of his sacrifice and his love for David to help him rise to his possibly rightful position after his father instead of becoming jealous over the possibility of some stranger taking his place is worthy of imitation. It is something that every person today should consider instead of fighting tooth and nail to block the way for others who want to advance.

I once read something that said: "Do you want your best friend to become your worst enemy? Overpass him/her. This is something that really happens. Sometimes relationships are maintained in the world if the power relations of one and the other are preserved, but when things are reversed, the relationship does not always hold.

What happens in the world is something that, if we neglect it, we also take it to the religious environment. It seems that the struggle to scale in a mundane way is something that we carry intrinsically in our DNA. It is the sin itself. Thank God that good biblical teachings help us understand that to be the first in the kingdom serving God, we must seek to be last (Mark 9:35). And with this attitude a great atmosphere is built in the church. With the different attitude, the church is destroyed from within.

I remember a sermon by Damian Jean-Baptist when we arrived with the missionary team in the Dominican Republic in 1994 with Angel Martinez as our missionary team leader. One warning that Damian gave us was to be very careful not to focus on wanting to occupy Angel's position. He warned us that our focus should be on being his helpers. Something similar happened to me before leaving Puerto Rico to join the team in the Dominican Republic. In my training to prepare to return as a missionary after only six months of being baptized and with a great risk of having adjustment problems, Robert Carrillo, an evangelist at the Church of Christ in Puerto Rico, warned me that my focus should be on serving others; take advantage of my knowledge of the Dominican Republic to help the other members of the team. And you know what? That was exactly what I did. Ha ha ha. This is a lie. I caused a lot of trouble. We say in the Dominican Republic, "I gave them a lot of water to drink".

My convictions when I became a disciple in Puerto Rico were very strong. However, I believed that all the churches worldwide should do everything exactly the same way. When I saw that things were not done in the Dominican Republic as I saw that they were done in Puerto Rico, I would fight a lot and expose it to others saying that things were not being done as they are done in Puerto Rico. That was a big burden for Angel and everyone else.

Another situation that led me to confrontations was trying to put into practice one of the teachings of the elder Joe Rodríguez, from the church in Los Angeles for leaders of the church in Puerto Rico. He taught us that as leaders we should be aware of each of the details of the things that were happening in the church; that we could not plead ignorance about what was happening in the church. We had to be aware of how the growth was going, how the contribution was going and many other details. As a good apprentice, when I returned to the Dominican Republic, I normally asked the person in charge of managing the contribution about how it was going. This was a heavy burden for her. She believed that I was doing it on suspicion of mismanagement. But I wasn't. Angel Martinez asked me and understood what I was doing and asked me to ask him directly instead of asking her. Thank God I learned a lot and I'm still learning.

> *Jonathan shows us his great trust in God.*

In a world in which, since ancient times, most people seek to protect their image and climb to high positions at any cost, Jonathan leaves us a great legacy. He shows his heart to serve and help David and also his great trust in God. In 1 Samuel 16 he is shown when David is consecrated king of Israel. Jonathan, instead of joining his father Saul's fight to destroy David, he understood God's plan and, against his father's will, protected him (1 Samuel 20).

There are several examples where the situation in the world is shown. I remember the film Gladiator with Russell Crowe (Maximus); "The Crown", the Netflix series; and situations experienced by me in work environments. These situations are pathetic of the fighting for power, also using power and trickery to try to climb positions or defend a status many times at the expense of the sacrifice of another person. It is the complete opposite of what we learn from the example of Jonathan's life.

In the first case with the film the Gladiator, the zeal of Commodus, the king's son, is seen, where he even kills his father to inherit the crown and prevent his passage to Maximus, as his father wished. Then Commodus seeks to make life impossible for Maximus. That power struggle, after all, has its adverse consequences for those who seek it instead of humbly submitting to God's will. In the end, although he dies in combat in the coliseum after being treacherously wounded, he receives all the honours.

In the case of "The Crown", the kings, especially Queen Elizabeth II, are fighting to maintain the monarchy at all costs. Those fights had a negative impact for the monarchy. They wanted to protect the image of the royal family regardless of the consequences. This is a very different example from the one that Jonathan offers us. We can follow the course of history and we will see the results. I imagine they will be very different from what we see when a person humbles himself and then is exalted by God.

Thirdly, I want to refer to current situations. Despite all my mistakes and all my weaknesses as a person and as a disciple of Jesus, I understand that I have not reached the point of doing things to climb by my own means at the expense of the sacrifice of another. Of course, as a sinner, my worldly thoughts do not stop flowing, believing that I am better than others and that I can do things better than someone that God has arranged to put above me in terms of leadership. But adherence to the scriptures keeps me down to earth and, both in my professional affairs and in the church, I am reminded of the scripture that says that all authorities are set by God (Romans 13:1). That gives me relief and helps me focus on doing the work that God allows me to do and seek to flourish where God puts me, even in the most inhospitable places. And being happy where God has put me I have reaped great fruits. Obviously, I could continue reaping many more by strengthening my relationship with God, being more humble and serving those who lead me more, even though sometimes I don't understand the reason for many actions. It is a matter of trust.

> *..for there is no authority except that which God has established.*
> *-Romans 13:1*

I remember my attitude when I became a disciple and seeing others doing things in the church. I also wanted to do it for various reasons. One of them was my usual attitude of not being afraid to do things in public and being willing to do anything without shame and without fear, always thinking that I am capable of doing it. An example is participating in and giving Bible studies on basic principles. While others are afraid to do it as soon as they become disciples, I, on the contrary, always thought that I was already capable of doing it, even though when the other person did it they did not understand anything because they did not do it properly. Something similar happened to me when I was part of the choir at my university in my engineering studies. Almost immediately upon my admission we had a concert and, although I was not quite ready with the sheet music for the songs, I was willing to sing. That shocked the director. What he normally saw was the opposite, people afraid to go on stage.

As for doing things in the church, since there were very few people in the church in Puerto Rico, from the beginning I had the responsibility as an usher helping direct people to their seats, especially the guests. But I also wanted to do other things, like preaching. Why? At first, it was partly to show my pride as a speaker. It wasn't until my heart changed in attitude that God began to use me on a level far beyond what I expected. So much so that, as we say here in the Dominican Republic, I had to "ask for cocoa," that is, I had to ask to be released from some of the activities because I felt that it was too much of a burden for me.

Something that God put on my heart once and I did it was to pray to help at least one person to become a Christian and then for that person to help me spiritually. I did it with more than one person. It was challenging, as thoughts occurred to me that I was possibly not growing spiritually enough, but the experience was very rewarding in terms of my humility. I understood that God was answering my prayers. I prayed for him because I understood that for the growth of the church, we need people who can grow more than we do. It is good that those of us who are here grow, but if those who come grow more, that benefits the kingdom and glorifies God. Those relationships helped me build great friendships, showing that our focus is not on glorifying ourselves, but on glorifying God.

Regarding the work environment, the focus to write about Jonathan and his attitude is also because of everything I have experienced in various work environments. I feel I have made my contributions and reaped the rewards of helping people below me to grow and then those people, including my students, have risen in experience and professional results to be above me. And the attitude that those people, although they are at a higher level, have towards me is as if I were far above them. At least, that's what I feel about the good relationships we cultivate.

On the other hand, I have also suffered when seeing what is normally done in this world. The Bible is not wrong when it says that all toil and all achievement spring from one person's envy of another (Ecclesiastes 4:4). This is opposite of the example of Jonathan. Again, without wanting to present myself as someone perfect, God has given me the ability with my academic training and now with my accumulated experience to be able to make good contributions in the work environment in which he has allowed me to be. However, due to a certain naivety, especially at the beginning, I hoped that this would be a reason for others around me to appreciate it and also appreciate what I could do for others.

> *All toil and all achievement spring from one person's envy of another.*
> -Eclesiastes 4:4

To my surprise, and possibly this should not have surprised me, in many cases it was the opposite. My success, and sometimes my appreciation for my superiors, aroused the envy of others.

On certain occasions I thought that everything was going well around me with my companions until the bomb exploded. I never heard it, but sometimes I have thought that keeping myself isolated to avoid the gossip that arose in certain environments and subordinates towards superiors, could imply that I could be a gossip from my colleagues towards the boss. But even a boss when I didn't support his blatant lies, while the other colleagues did, could come to think that I could be a snitch with his superiors. The attitude shown by a particular person towards me made me understand that. But that same person was the one who called me into his office one day to ask me to please pray for him. Even though I didn't agree with his way of thinking and doing unethical things, he did understand that I was submitting to God and doing things for his glory and not to please men.

In the end, Jonathan was killed in battle along with Saul, his father. He suffered the consequences of the bad behaviour of his father, but he left us a great legacy. His support for David was unconditional and it showed his faith in God. The Bible does not say what finally happened to him. My hope is that because of his convictions he was also a person faithful to God in everything. David, as his great friend, suffered when he died. David did not forget to protect his family when he showed him with Mephibosheth (2 Samuel 9), Jonathan's son, when he called him to his palace, returned everything that belonged to his family, and sat him down to eat forever at the king's table.

Jonathan's example is commendable. How much we need someone like him today in our society! How much harmony could we have! God has called us to put the scriptures into practice and to be multipliers of good examples. Let us maintain our good spiritual convictions and be multipliers of these good examples.

TO REFLECT

1. What attitude would you take towards someone who makes your life miserable in your environment because you maintain your convictions of righteousness towards God?

2. What would you do if you had been in the same situation as Jonathan?

3. What do you think made Jonathan have such an attitude in favor of David swimming against the current of that time and of history?

4. What attitude are you going to have?

X

The Poor Widow: Practical Faith

"...but she, out of her poverty, put in everything—all she had to live on."

- *MARK 12:44b*

The story of the poor widow is one of the best examples of giving sacrificially to God. This example is so great that if we are not careful enough, each person chosen to give a message for contribution for the poor could select the same scripture on this poor widow. I saw this happen while I was a preteen coordinator. Every week, someone would go to that class to give a contribution message. And every time, when someone was going to give the message, the other helper and I looked at each other and laughed. I imagine that the children wondered if there was no other scripture or perhaps, they thought it was customary to repeat the same one in church.

This scripture is a great example of sacrifice and giving, but what many people don't see when we give to those in need is that this is a great example of practical faith. I saw this approach in a class on benevolence offered by Estuardo Vásquez, director of HOPE *worldwide*

Guatemala based on the book Mighty Man of God. Giving to God really tests our faith. We give to help others, but at the end of the day, those who benefit are the ones who give. Serving those in need is a blessing for us. There are many scriptures that support that. When we trust the scriptures serving those in need is an act of faith.

The Bible inspires us to serve those in need and to sacrifice ourselves in the same way that Jesus did for us. We must do it just for serving and not for the benefit we will receive. Doing it to receive blessings may not have any merit. However, we cannot forget the automatic blessings that our service to those in need brings.

What I am saying is very similar to what we do by obeying our God and trusting him. Many people do not trust God because they do not believe in the promises of the Bible. If they trusted these promises, many people could come to Jesus. Sometimes people don't believe because of all the distortions that exist about the Scriptures and the Christian life. The religious world today and throughout history is responsible for the fact that many people do not believe. Many people who claim to be Christians do it only with their mouths without being an example like Jesus.

Trusting the scriptures serving those in need is a great act of faith.

If a some people decide to obey God for the reward they will receive, I believe God will not reject them. To do so is to show that they in fact trust God. It shows their faith. In the same way, we show our faith when we serve those in need, even if it is seeking to receive a reward from God. That is practical faith. My opinion is that it doesn't matter the reason why we do it, but we are doing it and glorifying God.

When the poor widow gave everything she had to live, she showed her strong faith. Such was her impact that she called Jesus' attention above all other people who gave, but that did not represent a true sacrifice. They gave from what was left over. She, on the other hand, gave everything she had to live (Mark 12.41-44, Luke 21: 1-4).

When it comes to giving and showing my faith, I would like to find heroes in our church. I am not the one, and I must confess it. I would like to be one. I want to be one of those heroes who are willing to give every drop of what they have. For our church in the Dominican Republic, I could take pride in giving and supporting it, but not necessarily with the sacrifice that is required. I usually give out of the much that God has given me. I feel blessed by God to allow me to usually have well-paying jobs, although at times I have been without any. And sometimes, when I run out of funds, my focus has been on meeting my needs and letting my contribution wait for the next payment. I have been a long way from giving to the level of the poor widow and showing my faith in that regard.

> *It is more blessed to give than to receive.*
> -Acts 20:35

The Bible does not say what happened next with the poor widow. But I can state that God gave her a special place in heaven. I ask the same question about other cases, such as the widow of Zarephath (1 Kings 17:8-16) and the situation of the Shunammite widow who fed Elisha (2 Kings 4). As it happened in these cases, I consider that God provided for the poor widow by showing her great faith and giving all that she had.

The ministry of Jesus did not focus only on the spiritual needs of people, but also on their physical needs (Matthew 9:23). He taught in the synagogues and also healed people of all ailments. The Scriptures also refer to the words of Jesus when he said that it is more blessed to give than to receive (Acts 20:35). And that is a reality. We feel the joy of giving, but we must also feel privileged when we are in the position of giving because it means that we have something to give and not a need to receive.

Several other scriptures in the Bible, both in the Old and New Testaments, support these points about how giving to those in need shows our faith. Deuteronomy 15:10-11 talks about giving generously to the poor and not grudgingly and the blessings that this brings. Others talk about having compassion for the poor and the happiness it gives us (Proverbs 14:21, Proverbs 22:9).

I would like to finish by referring to the scripture that says: *"Do not store up for yourselves treasures on earth, where moths and vermin destroy, and where thieves break in and steal. 20 But store up for yourselves treasures in heaven, where moths and vermin do not destroy, and where thieves do not break in and steal. 21 For where your treasure is, there your heart will be also."* (Matthew 6:19-21). I also point out that we must keep in mind that a loan to the poor is a loan to the Lord and that he himself will pay it back (Proverbs 19:17). Let us show our faith by serving those in need and giving to God sacrificially and not from what is left over, either out of love for the needy or the kingdom or because we hope to reap the benefits of our actions. Whatever the reason is for us to give, we show our faith in God as described in the Scriptures.

TO REFLECT

1. How strong is your faith as measured by what you do for those most in need?

2. Do you sacrifice when you give to others or give leftovers?

3. Where are you sowing, on earth or in heaven?

4. How balanced is your ministry in serving others with their physical and spiritual needs?

XI

Cloud of Witnesses: Living Examples

"Therefore, since we are surrounded by such a great cloud of witnesses, let us throw off everything that hinders and the sin that so easily entangles. And let us run with perseverance the race marked out for us, fixing our eyes on Jesus, the pioneer and perfecter of faith...."

- *HEBREWS 12:1-2*a

Through out this book we have seen many biblical examples of people who inspire us to continue to be faithful to our God despite our suffering and the tough situations we have faced. Although it is not included directly in this book to limit its size, I could also include additional examples of other people of faith described in Hebrews 11. Does that mean that the examples that inspire us are only in the Bible and that there are no others? No. The list does not end. Others are still living.

I originally thought about including only one additional living example in this chapter. However, later I thought it was more helpful to have testimonials from various living people who have been an inspiration to me and to others. These living examples can inspire us to do the same when we need to overcome obstacles in our walk with God. These are tangible people of flesh and blood. People who continue to fight in the spiritual battlefield and to help other people stay faithful. These people may be around us, but we don't always take advantage of their testimonies, or those testimonies are not always shared. I'm sure any of these people could have written this book instead of me. The fact that I am writing it is only because it seems that God has injected something into my veins that has inspired me to write and allows me to enjoy the process.

In the same way, there are many examples around the world, especially from people who live in places where Muslims are the majority or where Christianity is prohibited. In the book "Crazy for Jesus" we can see many testimonies of people who have given their lives to persevere in their walk with God despite the opposition. Let's see some testimonies from living people.

Milena: an anonymous hero

Milena? And where is that name in the Bible? Yes, it is. At least it is handwritten on a copy of the Bible. In which? In my mom's Bible. I am also sure that her name is written for eternity in the book of life. It is the promise that God makes to us, and my mother has understood it very well.

Once I was describing a testimony about my dad and his perseverance. At that time, it looked like I was leaving my mother out and not valuing her. However, I promised that later I was going to make sure I gave her the deserved honour. Well, I think this is the moment to do it.

Why an anonymous hero? Because of everything my mother has faced in life, beginning with the death of her mother when she was only five years old and what she has faced in her marriage to my dad; I consider this to be the most suitable title.

But, Wagner, isn't it better if you continue to focus on Biblical matters and save this narrative for another type of book? Someone might think this way. But what I am going to tell you here can be a great testimony that can help us persevere in our walk with God. My mother, despite following my dad in his unbelief, was one of the first people who became a disciple at the beginning of our mission in the Dominican Republic. Her example can really inspire us. I hope you don't think I am biased.

My mother's testimony about persevering to see blessings in her marriage is inspiring. Like any other woman, my mother had longed for a marriage in which her husband was truly her husband, not anyone else's. Unfortunately, the problem of unfaithfulness in the Dominican Republic is huge. In the countryside in the Dominican Republic, it is normal for a man to have more than one sentimental partner. It seems as if women are worthless. Sometimes, and I have seen it in my relatives, a man could have more than one woman living together and going to the farm to work together. I saw it with my father. In addition to the other women with whom my dad had children after "getting married" to my mother, he had another official public partner.

Although my father and my mother got together to create a family in 1962, they were not legally married until 1978. And this was not because they wanted to, but because it was a requirement of the Ministry of Education, when my mother began to work as a primary school teacher.

In spite of the unfaithfulness and my mother's suffering, she never abandoned my father. She remained faithful to him. She did it out of fear of having to raise a family without a father, as she later told me. Regardless of the reason, she persevered. And for her perseverance, God blessed her. Her long-awaited dream of having a real husband came true. My dad started to study the Bible the same week our mission team arrived in Santo Domingo, just before the first church service.

One of the challenges for my father was to be faithful to his wife and break the extramarital relationship he had. My dad took the challenge. He was baptized at the age of 54. Almost a year later, my mother was also baptized. This is how my mother's longed-for dream of having a husband came true. He also became a faithful husband who loves God above all else. Considering that, would you be willing to persevere until you see a long-awaited dream come true?

Juan Carlos Polanco: a new professional focus to do God's will

With a potential for a good professional and financial life, maybe higher than any of us who know him, Juan Carlos Polanco left his law studies at one of the best universities in the Dominican Republic. He went to live in New York and there he was invited to study the

Bible. Impacted by the life of Jesus, his desire was always to return to his country, the Dominican Republic, to help his people to know God.

His life at the university was a little different than many of ours. With more resources than many of us and training in another language that allowed him to have a job and generate income, his economic potential was huge. He could be compared to many of his friends, who are now very wealthy.

Juan Carlos returned from New York as part of the missionary team sent by the church there to start the one in the Dominican Republic. With his dream of being a lawyer, he tried to resume the pursuit of his law degree. Unfortunately, due to the university's policy of not recognizing the credits of someone who has been out for more than five years, that dream was destroyed. This was painful for him and for the friends around him. However, by God's grace and his promises to give more than what we sacrifice for him, Juan Carlos today is one of the evangelists of the International Church of Christ in the Dominican Republic, leading the Church in Santiago de los Caballeros. Through this, Juan Carlos can say with great satisfaction that his dream of helping many people in need, which he wanted to do by studying law, has come true.

As a minister in the church, Juan Carlos has faced many obstacles, like all of us, and he has overcome them to persevere in his walk with God. Juan Carlos has helped many people to reach come to the kingdom and stay faithful. The fact that I am faithful today is due, in part, to all the help I received from him. I am married to my beautiful wife Guarina and have two adorable daughters because of the advice he gave me to open my eyes and focus on the spiritual beauty of my wife. That also led me to see her physical beauty later.

When we become Christians, we sometimes have stereotypes of people who we think can easily become Christians and those who can't. Looking back, Juan Carlos is one of those people whom I would have considered difficult to become a disciple. But when God calls us, sincere hearts respond. He is the person with the most convictions for God that I have met. We were also students together at the same university campus, PUCMM in Santiago de los Caballeros.

Juan Carlos continues to give a powerful testimony of what it means to leave the world behind and focus totally on God. After failing with his marriage before being a Christian, he now has a great family devoted to God and supporting him to continue taking the message to different corners of the Dominican Republic.

Angel Martinez: leave your country and your family…

Just as God called Abraham and told him to leave his land and his family to go to an unknown place, so he told Angel Martinez. Potential members of the mission team for the Dominican Republic were meeting and having devotionals to get ready to depart, but Angel Martinez was not in the equation.

Angel is from the United States with a Puerto Rican father and a Dominican mother. He was born in Brooklyn, New York, and did not know the Dominican Republic. After becoming a disciple in New York, he went through different trials, to the point of being in critical spiritual situations. However, God had already chosen him beforehand to go to the Dominican Republic. God had chosen him not only to be part of the mission team but also to be its leader.

Since we arrived, Angel, along with his wife Luz, has been an example of stability and perseverance in their walk with God. If I talked about Juan Carlos' help to me, Angel is not far behind. At the beginning of the mission, and still is, when I went through critical situations, similar to his in New York, Angel was a valuable help to me. His deep convictions, his perseverance in helping me, and his example moved me to be also radical to persevere in my walk with God.

But God tests us with different situations to see how grateful we are to him and how pleased we are with what he gives us. God gave children to his friends around him, but not to him. Today, over forty years old, Angel and Luz are enjoying having their first child. This has happened as if it was by the work and grace of the Holy Spirit.

Under the direction of Angel, guided by the Holy Spirit, our church in the Dominican Republic has grown and been strengthened. In addition, over his shoulders is the responsibility of overseeing the churches in the Caribbean. Because of his convictions and his example, not only the churches in the Caribbean but also many churches in the world would like to "steal" him from the church in the Dominican Republic. Requests for him to serve in other churches are a lot. He keeps traveling practically all around the world. I hope that his child is an unintentional, but justified excuse for him to stay at home in the Dominican Republic.

Amauris Brea: come back to your land, it needs you.

Nooooooo…. Please… Such an expression could very well have come from Amauris Brea's mouth. However, it was completely the opposite. When God called him to return to his land, he answered to that calling. And he did it with conviction.

Before going to live in New York while he was still young, Amauris was just another street child in the Dominican Republic. He suffered and wandered the streets trying to survive. He went with his mother to live in New York and could very well decide to never look back. And doesn't God ask us not to look back? Yes, that's how it is. But he also asks us to serve him when needed.

When God called him, he accepted the calling. He studied the Bible, put aside his friends who did not help him (many of them may be dead today), forgot about his focus on getting material stuff, and accepted to walk with Jesus. Later, not long after, when God called him back to his country, he accepted it. To any other people, this decision could be scary. He may have thought that he could expect a life of suffering on the streets of Santo Domingo again. That was his life before during his childhood. Ah! Actually, it was not different when he came back. He came back to the streets again. But this time, it was with a new focus. Now he is living on the streets evangelising, seeking more people to come to God. Like the other missionaries who came to the Dominican Republic, often Amauris didn't have food to eat. But that didn't kill the joy he had helping his people in his homeland. On the other hand, that strengthened him.

Originally, Amauris was also very helpful in helping me strengthen my convictions and persevere. Later, it was him and his wife who helped me and my wife overcome many obstacles in our marriage.

Because of his approach and evangelism, Amauris was tireless and a great example. And he continues to be. It was normal for me to invite people to church and to study the Bible, and they would tell me that they had already been invited. And when I asked who invited them, the obvious answer came: Amauris. This happened to me one time at about 5:00 a.m. I invited someone in a public car and, to my surprise…well, not so much, he told me that Amauris had already invited him.

Amauris has been an inspiration to many people in strengthening their convictions and in their prayer life. Frequently, Amauris told us, that he would rather have a group of people who pray and rely on God instead of having a group making an extraordinary effort to achieve their evangelistic goals on their own. Prayer brings us closer to God and makes our goals come true.

Amauris continues to be a pillar in our family of churches helping many other people to persevere with his example and his teachings. In addition to taking care of his family and having a full-time professional job, he had the responsibility of running one of our churches in Santo Domingo. Recently, he moved back to the United States.

I would also like to mention that when Amauris returned to the country, he did not have university training. He only had his high school diploma. In addition to having to work to survive, Amauris took the challenge of enrolling in the university. He originally started, but different circumstances made him stop. However, his vision of getting a college degree didn't die. He kept his hope alive. Years later he was able to graduate with a degree in Business Administration. That has helped him to be able to have a good professional job to support his family and not be a burden to the church, just as Paul did. This also helped him to be able to challenge other people or students to do the same.

Luz Martinez: an example of love for Jesus

I met Luz Martinez (Luz Paulino Difó, maiden name) when I arrived in Puerto Rico in December 1993. She was one of the people who warmly welcome me to the church. She made sure that I saw an example of what it meant to put the love of Jesus into practice. She was one of those disciples who overflowed me with the love of Jesus. It was a feeling beyond explanation. Then, I began to understand that this love only came from people who remain in Jesus (John 15:1-10).

It is true that no one can remain faithful in their walk with God if their focus is not on Jesus and remaining in him. If our trust is not placed in him, at some point we will fall. But it is also true that the example of other people in the kingdom helps us to persevere. In the same way that there are many people disappointed and reluctant to come to church because of the bad example they see with many people who call themselves Christians without walking at the feet of Jesus, so also good examples are like a magnet to attract others and help them to persevere.

Luz's trust in a sinner like me is something that, in addition to my focus on Jesus, helps me to persevere. Sometimes I can be not so spiritual and lose sight of Jesus and maybe get into trouble. However, knowing that I will constantly be face to face with people like her, who are an example and who appreciate me, is also another motivation not to sin and to stay away from problems that could take me away from God.

In addition to the initial shock I received in Puerto Rico, I also saw the example of Luz's service. Possibly, she never noticed that I was watching. But the example I saw in her was worthy of imitation. As an unpaid intern for the church in Puerto Rico, helping Raúl Vásquez with his administrative work and Robert and Michelle Carrillo with whatever they needed, including taking the car to the carwash and filling the gas tank, I had to go to their house frequently. When I needed to go, I always saw Luz taking care of their daughters, Elena and Alexis. She was serving humbly. It was an imitation of the serving approach of Jesus. God was preparing her to lay the foundation for everything she does now helping many other women.

Her impact on my life continued in Santo Domingo when I was honoured to be part of the same mission team to plant the church. I had many people who trusted in me. In the case of Luz, I understand that her trust exceeds the limits. That is a great inspiration not to fail in my walk with God. And don't get me wrong. If our focus is not on Jesus, we are going to fall. But the example of other people around us is also a strong inspiration to persevere. The women in the church are the best testimony of what I say. They have received that support and have seen Luz as a living example.

Sometimes we see people and we don't know their lives in depth. We think that many people remain faithful to God because of all the blessings that God has given them. We think of someone like Job before God took away all his possessions and even his health beyond explanation. But when we learn more about the difficult situations that other people have faced, we are more inspired to persevere.

I am grateful that Luz was willing to share a little about her life in this book. This should also be an example to imitate and to put aside any situation from the past to focus on living for Jesus and glorifying our God. This is what Luz tells us.

"My name is Luz Martinez. I was born on January 29, 1969. I was born in the province of María Trinidad Sánchez (Nagua). I am the youngest daughter of my parents, Hipólito Paulino and Herminia Difó. I am the wife of a wonderful man named Angel Martinez.

I spent the first years of my life on a beautiful mountain with my paternal grandmother and my brothers. I consider myself a loving person, with empathy, helpful, with a genuine interest in others, and a deep desire to leave my footprints wherever I go.

I have been a minister since I was 21 years old. Prior to that, I worked as a cashier, secretary, and student advisor. I have travelled a lot. I have given conferences for women, marriage, and students internationally since 1994. I have achieved all of this with a lot of effort and with the help of my God, since in my first years of life, I did not have a firm base or much stability. I studied basic education at El Factor de Nagua High School, in San Francisco de Macorís, and high school in New York City. As you can see, I didn't have a life long enough to establish my roots anywhere. That was until knowing about God.

But I want you to see how God's love transformed my life when I was 19 years old. At that age, I was converted and baptized, while I was in my sophomore year of college, at the New York City Church of Christ.

Studying the Bible, seeing the love of Jesus for me, the mercy of God and the love of the brothers in the church saved me from the destruction towards which I was leading my life. I had just arrived in the United States, and it was a very difficult time for me. I was very lonely, without friends, with a very troubled mind, full of bitterness, anger, frustration, and confusion, as my father, who was an alcoholic all his life, had committed suicide just nine months ago.

My parents moved to the United States when I was four years old. It took them eleven years to get the documents to take me to live with them. The blow of losing the father that I had been hoping to have for so many years affected me tremendously. I fell into a clinical depression for which I should have been treated but was not. Many times, I wished to die. I felt that life had no meaning to me and that it was not worth living.

My life was filled with uncertainty, insecurity, lies, impurity, selfishness, and pride. I spent my days cheating and being cheated on. By the time they invited me to study the Bible, I was already tired of a life that had just begun. I was empty, sad, and without a purpose. I tried to find refuge in boyfriends, work, studies, and *parties. But those things did not fill the emptiness that I had in my life. It wasn't until I sought refuge in God's word that I found peace in my soul.*

Almost 25 years ago I made the decision to live a life to glorify God, to give value to the cross of Christ, and honour his sacrifice. Not a single day has passed in which I have not seen God's love and mercy for me.

For 19 years now, my husband and I have had the privilege of serving as pastors in a church that truly loves us and that we also love, the Santo Domingo Church of Christ in the Dominican Republic. God has given us four beautiful foster daughters and two beautiful little grandchildren.
About six years ago, God made it possible for us to build our little house with the help of many friends, family, and a couple at church. In the last 19 years, God has given us the privilege of being missionaries, training other missionaries, planting churches, and restoring others. God has given us the privilege of working with a team of ministers who truly love God, God's people, and love us too. Both my husband and I are eternally grateful to God for showing so much mercy and protection to us. That's why every day I feel like the psalmist felt when he said: "Whom have I in heaven but you? And earth has nothing I desire besides you. My flesh and my heart may fail, but God is the strength of my heart and my portion for ever…But as for me, it is good to be near God. I have made the Sovereign Lord my refuge…(Psalm 73:25-26 and 28a). And I'm sure it is for you too.

My hope is that each one of you can see the love of God in your life every day as I have seen it."

What is your personal testimony? Is there a burden that you keep carrying that does not let you see the glory of God in your life to the fullest?

Jesus Cruz: in spite of his unbelief

When Jesus was still a teenager, our sisters in Puerto went to his house to study the Bible with his sister. The focus of this Puerto Rican teenager was simply to annoy the sisters. This may have seemed as if his heart was hard and far from knowing God. Then his sister became a disciple and Jesus became interested in studying the Bible. Soon he also became a disciple at the age of 18. Later, he became a great man of God and a man of deep spiritual convictions.

Jesus is one of my best friends, despite the distance and the passing of years. With less than a year of being a disciple, Jesus was one of my inspirations when I became a disciple in Puerto Rico. His love for God and his dedication to always rely on the Bible and prayer, as well as his focus on helping other people through the teaching of the Bible, helped me deepen my convictions about what it really meant to be a disciple of Jesus. As I mentioned before, Jesus was subtle in helping me overcome obstacles of discouragement and homesickness when I had to stay in Puerto Rico after being baptized to later go with the mission team to Santo Domingo.

It was obvious that people like Jesus Cruz would remain faithful despite seeing others falling away. Of all the disciples with whom we were sharing the house in El Escorial in Puerto Rico, only a few have persevered. Those of us who have persevered have done so by sticking to our Bibles, to prayer, and doing the work for God regardless of the cost. Jesus Cruz is one of those disciples.

Jesus Cruz, and what a spiritual name!, leads our church in Puerto Rico. Along with his wife Mirels, they continue to help many people to remain faithful or to come to God on the Isla del Encanto, Puerto Rico. Precisely, the first Bible talk that I attended in Puerto Rico was on campus, and it was led by Jesus and Mirels. Although there was no special sentimental focus between them, later God made them see that he had created them for each other.

Like the other cases I have mentioned here in this chapter, the testimony of Jesus is living. Following Jesus himself gives us his testimony.

"I grew up in a world where people talk about God. As a child, I was "baptized" by my parents, as is the custom in our Puerto Rican culture. I went to a church with my aunt. When I was a teenager, my parents started going to a church where it was taught that a prophet received a gold plate with a new message for the world. They imposed their hands on me and I experienced all things done in the religious world. But all I was doing was to my disappointment and pain. With all that, I did not see a good path for my life. I was lost, aimless, alone, distraught, and wondering if this was what life was all about.

As a 17-year-old, I began to try to understand the purpose of my life. In that process, I went in search of girls, alcohol, money, and all kinds of satisfaction of the flesh. Disappointed in that search and losing hope, every day I was more into each of these things. I thought I needed more women, more alcohol, and more money. But everything was getting worse. The disappointment and the pain were growing. It was like being in some kind of vicious circle with no way out. I remember running out of strength thinking about how I could get out of there. But I didn't see any other way to live.

I remember lying on my bed and looking at the ceiling after coming home drunk from a nightclub and wondering what I could offer my children if I had a family and what I would be like as a father. I was looking for the answer and began to cry, not being able to find it. But even so, I continued to live as I understood life should be. Actually, what I was doing was not living, but surviving.

One Sunday morning, my sister Ivellisse knocked on my door to invite me to church. I heard the invitation and my heart said yes, but my pride and my disappointment with churches said no. For seven months, every Sunday she persistently knocked on the door. One day, when she least expected it, and by God's work in his perfect plan, two sisters came to study the Bible with my mother. From a distance, I listened to what they were talking about. I heard something that shocked me. It was the scripture in Matthew 28:18-19 about going to all nations to make disciples. I approached them to ask if this is not the exclusive responsibility of a pastor or priest. They, with all their love, explained to me the scripture that this is the responsibility of every man and every woman who wants to be a Christian or a disciple of Jesus. At that moment, I found the starting point of knowing where to look for something else for my life.

I remember my first visit to the church. I came to a place where I didn't know anyone and they welcomed me as if I were part of their lives. I saw open gates of trust. I saw sincere friends. I saw that my life had found something I was looking for. I remember hearing that sermon of the paralysed man, the man lowered by his friends from the roof of a house that was not his. But what impacted me the most was that I didn't fall asleep during the sermon. They invited me to study the Bible and to learn how to have a relationship with God. What is this about having a relationship with God? I asked myself. With my heart so hardened by the blows of life, I couldn't see that everything I experienced was something that God himself was preparing for my heart to meet him.

I started studying scriptures one after another. I delved into them and my heart beat more and more to know the God that I had never known. Then, there was a study where my heart was broken. The study is titled "The Cross." I was able to see clearly through the Scriptures all that Jesus did for us, but especially for me. In my childhood, I listened, I watched movies, and I was saturated with information, but without any emotional connection. I didn't have a clear understanding that if I were the only being on this planet, Jesus would still sacrifice his life for me.

I had never had a connection to the death of Jesus in that way. From that moment on, I saw clearly not only what it is to have a relationship with God, where I communicate with him in prayer and listen to his word, but also to know that he paid the ultimate price for me on the cross. Since that moment, I have made the best decision, at only 17 years old, but with a great love that drove me and still drives me to this day, to be the man God wants me to be."

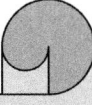

TO REFLECT

1. And your testimony, what is it?

2. What have you had to sacrifice to show your love for God and persevere?

3. What obstacle are you trying to overcome?

4. What paradoxical situation in your walk with God have you experienced and that in the end you have seen the blessings?

XII

Fully Trusting in Your God

"Trust in the Lord and do good; dwell in the land and enjoy safe pasture. Take delight in the Lord, and he will give you the desires of your heart."

- *PSALMS 37:3-4*

In our lives as Christians, we will face difficult situations. Many people think that it is impossible to overcome all of them. When we see biblical and living examples of people who have faced similar situations, it increases our faith.

A relationship with God is not a relationship without suffering. We suffer, but God promises that we will not go through situations beyond what we can bear and he gives us the way out (1 Corinthians 10:13). The good examples we see are also great tools to help us trust God. It doesn't matter how difficult the situation is, God always provides the way out. Don't expect him to eliminate suffering, but do expect him to give you the way out. He promises solutions to his faithful. He is also faithful to what he promises (Romans 15:8).

> *It doesn't matter how difficult the situation is, God always provides the way out.*

God's way of thinking is very different from ours. Our trust in God is sometimes weakened when we do not receive what we expect in our time. Even if this does not happen, we must trust. Sooner or later, God provides the solution. Many times, what he gives us is much more than what we expect. We will never receive less than expected even if we don't see it at the time.

I say that the Bible is the greatest love story ever written. God shows his love for his people from Genesis to Revelation. He also keeps all his promises. This helps us trust him. To have that confidence, we need to understand the Scriptures by sticking to them. Throughout the entire Bible, we see how his promises are fulfiled. This applies to the past, the present, and the future. Because of his love, God is willing to sacrifice anything (Jeremiah 30:11) for his people. To understand God, we must stick to his word. The examples of other people help us to know God better.

To understand God, we must stick to his word.

Describing all God's blessings for those people who trust him could be endless. For this reason, this book includes only a few examples. Here we present some of the blessings for those who trust.

God is a God of blessings. We see the great blessing since the creation of Adam when God gave Eve to him. He gave him a helper suitable for him (Genesis 2:18). It is true that God blesses us because he wants. He does it regardless of whether we trust him or not. He is sovereign. When we don't trust we can miss the blessings. God can give them to us, but we may not see them. We may see what he gives us as a burden. The lack of trust in God can go that far. To get the blessings will also depend on whether we are ready to receive them or not. What we receive depends on our hearts and how we are going to administer such blessings.

God is a God of blessings. We see the great blessing given since the creation of Adam and Eve.

The simple fact of God giving us life and creating us in the way he did are more than enough blessings to be grateful. Sometimes we don't even appreciate life itself or we think we deserve everything. That should not be the case. We need to be grateful for what God has done for us. He has blessed us, and the more grateful we are, the more he continues to give us.

The greatest blessing that God has given us, despite how sinful we are, has been Jesus. From the very beginning, he already had Jesus in mind to use him for the redemption of sin, and to give humanity the opportunity to return to him. However, the sacrifice of Jesus is foolish for many. For others it is the most powerful thing there is (1 Corinthians 1:18). That's for those who trust him. God knows what is best for us.

God knows what is best for us.

God also blessed Noah by allowing him to have many children to fill the earth. In his time, Noah was the only one who lived according to God's will. Noah went against the grain. He showed great faith and walked through the narrow gate. He was not dominated or led by the flock. He was willing to pay the price, and he had his rewards. Noah withstood everyone's mockery.

Abraham also trusted God. He was a descendant of Shem, the first son of Noah. All the blessings of humanity after the flood are Noah's. What he did was big. It is difficult to resists that a whole society goes one way and one a person goes against it. I have experienced that to a minimal degree in my academic and work environment. But that is nothing compared to what Noah had to face.

God continued to bless Noah through his descendants. He also blessed Abraham. Why? Because Abraham trusted him. God gives us free will to decide. When God called Abram (Abraham), he could make many excuses. However, Abram trusted and was obedient despite the strong challenge that God was giving him to leave his land, his relatives, and his father's house to go to an unknown place when he was seventy-five years old. Abram trusted God and God blessed him beyond expectations.

Noah withstood everyone's mockery.

Another aspect of trust in God that is highlighted in the life of Abraham is his trust in spite of not seeing what was being offered to him. He was not controlled by his emotions or his supposed personal strengths. He did not act according to his will, but according to God's will when he separated from Lot. Abraham himself proposed that him and Lot separate. As his uncle, Abraham could make the decision and tell Lot to go one way and that he would go the other. He could have taken what he considered to be best and leave Lot the worst. However, instead of making the decision, Abraham decided to leave it in God's hands. Lot made the decision acting as a human being. He acted on what his eyes saw. He took the land that looked best. Later, we can see all the problems that Lot faced. Originally, he was taken as a prisoner (Genesis 14:2-14) and later came the destruction of Sodom and Gomorrah (Genesis 19:1-27). Later, also came the situation of incest with his daughters, from where the Moabites and Ammonites emerged, peoples despised by God (Genesis 19: 31-38).

Abraham trusted God and got blessed him beyond expectation.

Abraham, on the other hand, left his decision in God's hands. Although it didn't look like the best decision, it was. And God blessed him. God gave him a good place to live. Abraham trusted God and got blessed beyond expectation. Because of his trust, God made him the father of the faithful and of all generations that are faithful to God.

In addition to specific blessings to different people, the Bible is full of different situations where we can see the great promises and blessings of God for those who trust in him. The people of Israel suffered in Egypt and God allowed it to train them. God understood who he was dealing with and all he had to work with them. God understood how sin had invaded the hearts of his people despite seeing so many blessings. This suffering gave them perseverance, perseverance gave them character, and character gave them hope, a hope that did not disappoint them (Romans 5:1-5).

The people of Israel suffered in Egypt, and God allowed it to train them.

In spite of all of Jacob's situations, he too was obedient to God and received his blessings. The first blessing that Jacob received was the changing of his name. After Jacob wrestled with the Angel of God and was victorious (Genesis 32: 22-32), God gave him the blessing to change his name to Israel. Jacob trusted God and God saw his heart. That fight was a difficult situation that he had to face and he did not give up until he received God's blessing. To receive God's blessings, we must trust him. Genesis 35 also describes how when God asks Jacob to go to Bethel and build him an altar, he did not hesitate to obey. Jacob sought to eliminate all the strange gods from among them and we see his gratitude to God for always accompanying him when he says: "—*Get rid of the foreign gods you have with you, and purify yourselves and change your clothes. 3 Then come, let us go up to Bethel, where I will build an altar to God, who answered me in the day of my distress and who has been with me wherever I have gone.*" (Genesis 35:2-3).

> *To receive God's blessings we must trust him.*

God's blessings and promises to Abraham continue to be fulfilled through the blessings to Jacob. Let's keep in mind that God knew what he did when he chose Jacob. He understood that, despite all the cheating he did, Jacob was obedient. God is always seeking those hearts. We see the opposite with Esau, his brother (Genesis 27:41).

God's blessings continue through Joseph as he always had a good attitude toward God and all the difficult situations he faced. I think that any other person could have reacted very differently and filled his heart with bitterness.

Joseph's example is to be admired. From him, we learn many lessons to persevere in our walk with God despite the trials we face. Genesis 37-50 talks about his story. The story inspires me. This is also very interesting for young single disciples who are struggling to persevere in the midst of so much wickedness that exists today and all the temptation to sexual sin. Well…and not just singles, but married people too.

God had definitely chosen Joseph for something great. Possibly, God saw his heart and convictions beforehand. Despite his arrogance and lack of wisdom to talk to his brothers, God blessed him because of the confidence he had. Joseph never doubted the plan that God had for him. In situations where many of us might have given up, Joseph stood firm with his convictions. He saw God working in his life despite all the adversities he faced.

Because of his faith and his perseverance, God blessed him beyond what he and any of us could have imagined. His focus was not on the pursuit of power or material ambitions. He simply wanted to stay faithful to God. In Joseph, the word unfaithfulness to God did not exist. For this reason, in a strange country and belonging to a strange race, God placed him as the second most im-

> *In Joseph the word unfaithfulness to God did not exist.*

portant person in Egypt. His perseverance in his walk with God had an impact on his family and on all the people of Israel, God's chosen people. He made the difference over his brothers. While in the hearts of his brothers, there was evil and bitterness, his was full of love and forgiveness. Joseph also went against the grain just like Noah.

Later, God also blessed his children, especially Ephraim. Just as he did with Jeremiah (Jeremiah 1: 4-5), God chose Ephraim before he realised it. He chose Ephraim not because of what he did, but because God wanted it. Ephraim was younger than his brother Manasseh, but Jacob put him above by giving him his blessing. Let's be prepared. When we persevere in our walk with God, we do not imagine all that God can do with each one of us.

> *God never gives us less than what we ask him with faith and what our eyes can see.*

Before I continue describing all these blessings, let me mention the incredible blessing that God gave Jacob to allow him to see his son Joseph again, whom he considered to be dead. Jacob was a faithful person to God and God blessed him. But, possibly, the greatest blessing he could receive, or at least the greatest emotionally, was seeing his son Joseph practically resurrected. For Jacob it was like a resurrection. I don't think the Bible mentions it, but it's likely that Jacob never stopped praying that God would allow him to see his son again, even if it was after his death. Possibly Jacob always had the hope of seeing him again and, because of that confidence, God gave him more than what he expected. This is the way our God works. He never gives us less than what we ask of him or what our eyes can see.

> *We need to trust to continue to receive blessings.*

Ephraim's blessing above his brother Manasseh and all other relatives to continue the promises of God to his ancestor Abraham, comes by God's decision. Ephraim didn't have to do anything about it. He also teaches us great lessons.

Sometimes we persevere in our walk with God because of the blessings we know we will receive, but it is also good to focus on the harsh consequences that come as a result of disobedience. This is clearly described in Deuteronomy 28. The first part describes everything that obedience brings. The second part, all the consequences of disobedience.

Initially, Ephraim was obedient to God. That is why God chose him and exalted him above all his relatives. God established his sanctuary in Ephraim, specifically in Shiloh. Shiloh was the special place where everyone had to go to praise God (Jeremiah 7:12). If we analyse the maps, Shiloh is right in the centre of the kingdom of Israel. It was the central point and the special place to praise God.

But, despite everything that God did with Ephraim, his chosen tribe, they forgot about him. They were living a religious life and turned away from the God who had given them all blessings and power. They thought that the fact of merely having the ark of the covenant was enough (1 Samuel 4:3, 11 and 18). Their religious life without power led them to be defeated. It was not them themselves that expressly decided to turn away from God, but it was God who turned away from them (Psalms 78:58-61). It is as if an entire church has turned away from God. The group stayed together, but they were powerless. They continued to consider themselves as special people chosen by God (Hosea 9:16-17 and 11:1-4).

> *God never leaves us alone when we are carrying out his mission.*

Later you can see how the enemies, the Philistines, defeated the people of God (Ephraim). Never before had the people of Israel received a defeat. In our walk with God, we cannot be happy only with reaching the kingdom. We need to persevere and to continue to trust God to continue to receive his blessings.

In the history of religious groups, there have been situations in which groups have started with great power and dedication to God. However, their subsequent lack of convictions and focus has led to their downfall. They have focused on worshiping things created by God and not on worshiping the creator, God. Any group can make this mistake. To persevere, we must stay united to God and his son Jesus even if we need to sacrifice our own lives.

Because of Ephraim's lack of focus and disobedience, God, who always shows his compassion for his people, chose David and his beloved Mount Zion. And David took care of his people and led them with a skilful hand and with integrity of heart (Psalms 78: 65-

72). From that compassion of God by choosing David, we can see the results today.

We can also see God's blessings when he called Moses to guide his people. Moses was just taking care of the sheep of his father-in-law Jethro (Reuel). Moses was unsure if he could take the responsibility God was giving him. He focused on his weaknesses and not on the fact that God was with him. God never leaves us alone when we are carrying out his mission. God promised to be with Moses (Exodus 3:12). Let's go a little further back. Let's see how God was with Moses when he was a child facing the possibility of dying. Moses could not defend himself and God was the one who rescued him. God worked out a perfect plan to save him and then use him for his purpose.

God allowed his people to live in Egypt and to suffer there. However, God never abandoned them. God had his plan to show his power before a group of people who he had to shape their hearts to love him more, the Hebrew people, and other people who did not believe in him, the Egyptian. Possibly, nobody imagined that God could have the power to rescue a people plunged into slavery and with no hope in sight.

God protected his people in the desert.

Later, Moses could have given up trying to free the people talking to Pharaoh. The more difficult the situation, the more God showed his power. God himself worked with Pharaoh to make him more stubborn and to show his power. How do you feel when you have to face difficult situations similar to this one with the people we want to help change their attitude towards God? How much would you persevere?

God blesses us and wants us to always trust him until the end. Let's take the challenge and we will see the reward.

If Moses had not persevered, the people of Israel might still be living in slavery in Egypt. Later, God protected his people in the desert. He protected him from all bad weather, from wild beasts, he did not allow his clothes to wear out, he gave him food (manna and quail) and protected them from the other people. Have you been through similar situations in which you don't know if you are going to survive?

In the desert their situation was so difficult that they wanted to return to Egypt. Many lost their faith. What do you think would have happened to the people if they had gone back into slavery? But, out of love for his people, God preferred to kill those who did not have faith and wanted to return, to carry out his purpose with those who truly trusted him. Notice that those who went ahead were younger. What lesson can we learn from this?

We can continue writing about all the acts of God accompanying his people, but if I describe everything, just as John says (John 21:25), even the whole world would not have room for the books that would be written. Or this book would become so big that it would be impossible to carry and, instead of helping inspire someone to persevere, it would be another obstacle in the way.

All these examples of God's love and blessings should inspire us to trust him. I have presented examples in the Bible and examples of living people. God does not abandon us. God blesses us and wants us to always trust him until the end. Let's take the challenge and we will see the reward. Let's trust him until our last breath.

TO REFLECT

1. Have you ever been tempted to give up and stop trusting God because you didn't see his blessings in your life?

2. Reflect on God's blessings in your life and share them to inspire others.

3. What factors do you consider that can prevent you from not trusting and that you need to fight with the tools that God puts in your hands?

4. Stick to the Scriptures and live a life of prayer and commitment to trust God.

ABOUT THE AUTHOR

Wagner Méndez was a missionary to his own country, the Dominican Republic. After becoming a Christian in Puerto Rico, he received training and returned with a team of missionaries from New York City to start the Santo Domingo Church of Christ. After being in the church in Santo Domingo for almost twenty years, he moved with his family to be with the church in the city of Santiago de los Caballeros in the northern region of the Dominican Republic. In addition to his time dedicated to the church, Wagner is an agricultural economist and business consultant with more than thirty years of experience contributing to business development and entrepreneurship in the Caribbean. Currently, he is economic and commercial counsellor in the Embassy of the Dominican Republic in the United Kingdom.

Other Books Written by Wagner Méndez

All of them can be purchased at:
https://www.amazon.com/s?k=wagner+mendez&ref=nb_sb_noss

Printed in Great Britain
by Amazon